his

simple and sexy things to do
for the one you *love*

hers

Justin Cord Hayes *and* **Nicole Murn Hayes**

Adams Media
Avon, Massachusetts

Published by Adams Media, an F+W Publications Company
57 Littlefield Street
Avon, MA 02322
www.adamsmedia.com

ISBN: 1-59337-479-8

Printed in Canada.
J I H G F E D C B A

Library of Congress Cataloging-in-Publication Data
Hayes, Justin Cord.
His/hers : simple and sexy things to do for the one you love / Justin Cord Hayes
and Nicole Murn Hayes.
p.   cm.
Includes bibliographical references and index.
ISBN 1-59337-479-8
1. Couples—Miscellanea. 2. Man-woman relationships—Miscellanea.
3. Love—Miscellanea. 4. Marriage—Miscellanea. 5. Creative activities
and seat work. 6. Flip books. I. Title: Simple and sexy things to do for the one you love.
II. Hayes, Nicole Murn. III. Title.
HQ801.H3717 2005
306.7—dc22
2005021921

*This book is available at quantity discounts for bulk purchases.
For information, please call 1-800-872-5627.*

dedication

Justin would like to dedicate this book to his wife and partner, Nicole Hayes. I cherish our time together and look forward to many more years of romance.

acknowledgments

Justin would like to thank Jason Flynn, Paula Munier, and happy Hollywood endings.

his contents

❦

5

The Manly Art of Romance

men are good at many things: killing spiders, opening jars, lifting boxes. But romance? It's just not considered manly. You buy flowers only when you've screwed up royally. You believe cuddling is something you do when you hope it will lead to more intimate pursuits. And you think talking is something you do to convey information, not feelings.

But you can be taught! Remember when you finally started to put the seat down? Or when you started putting dirty clothes in a hamper, instead of on the floor? Or when you surrendered the remote for the very first time? Those were breakthroughs, avenues on the road to romance.

But why stop there? If you love someone, there's nothing more manly than letting her know it. First, learn these three words: "I," "love," and "you." Practice saying them. Get to where you can say them anytime, not just when food, sex, or stupid moves are involved. Then get ready to do something that will really put hair on your chest: Show her that you love her.

You're not sure how? Not to worry. If you're manly enough to overcome your aversion to reading directions, you can get a number of ideas in the next several pages. Most are easy and won't take much time away from televised sports. Even better, most of them are cheap or cost absolutely nothing. And yes, in case you're wondering: It's OK to make her think you made up every single one of the following romantic gestures.

1

Every picture tells a story

items you'll need for this romantic gesture are a photo album, snapshots from throughout your relationship, a pack of Post-it notes, and the raw courage necessary to be open and vulnerable (not sold in stores, sorry).

She asks you—all the time—to tell her why you fell in love with her, right? Then she actually expects you to come out with something brilliant in a split second. Geez, who does she think you are, William Frikkin' Shakespeare? Even he couldn't give you a sonnet on demand. But with this gesture, you can take the time to be really eloquent, and you'll get some help in the form of visual aids.

Look through the photos you've gathered throughout your time together. Find some that speak to you. Don't worry about what they say just yet. This is the manly, hunting-and-gathering part of the gesture.

Once you've found the photos you like, put them in the album. The order doesn't matter.

Now comes the hard part. Look at each photo and ask yourself this question: How does this picture remind me of why I love her? For example, if you chose a photo of her making a silly face, it's probably because you love the way she makes you laugh. Once you've answered the above question, write the answer on a Post-it. Stick the note on the photo. Do this for all the photos. In no time at all, you will create a lasting testament to your love for her.

This is an ideal Valentine's Day gift. It's a hell of a lot cheaper than a dozen roses, and it comes from the heart, so it will mean more to her than flowers.

2

Welcome to paradise

items you'll need for this gesture can vary, but two things are necessary: bubble bath stuff—the expensive kind—and lots of scented candles. You can add items like pink flamingos, a compact disc of Hawaiian music, some leis . . . anything that says "island paradise" to you. for this gesture to work, you'll need the element of surprise, so make sure when you get started she's out of the house but due home soon.

Whether she has a 9 to 5 job or works in the home, she's as busy and harried as you are. She'd love nothing more than for you to whisk her off spontaneously to a tropical island. You say you can't afford a stack of postcards, much less a trip below the equator? No problemo. You can bring paradise home.

First, put a note on the door that says, "Welcome home to paradise," or something like that. Then get the bathroom ready. Cover it in tropical paradise items, if you've bought them or if you are a connoisseur of kitsch and already have them lying around. Put the music on repeat. Then set up the candles around the room and light them. Finally, start a hot bath with plenty of those top-drawer bubbles.

When she comes home to this paradise-away-from-paradise, she will forget all about her cares of the day. Your chances of getting lucky after she pulls the plug on the bath are very good, but don't press that luck. Just let her relax if that's all she wants to do.

This gesture is good anytime. If she's been particularly stressed lately, it's the ideal time to send her to paradise.

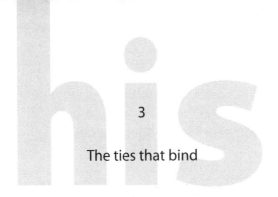

3

The ties that bind

for this gesture, all you need are a whole bunch of neckties.

If you're like most guys, you've got more than your share of neckties. You've got ties you've carried with you since high school, some worn only for long-ago job interviews, a few that have stains you can't pretend are part of the design. They make a mess of your closet, sliding off of tie racks like colorful spaghetti and creating untidy heaps on the floor that are often the subject of stern reprimands. She'll never yell at you about them again—well, at least not for a few days—if you make that mess into a simple romantic gesture.

Take your misfit ties and use them to spell words or shape hearts all along the floor. Sprinkle the living room in I ♥ U, connect this sentiment to UR 4 ME in the hallway. Make an unbroken string of loving sentiments and images that end—where else—at the bedroom, with you on the other side of the door. If she's followed your trail all the way to the end, then she's fit to be tied. There's a good chance you'll be making some whoopee amid the Windsor knots in no time.

This gesture is good for any workday, especially if she's been complaining about the stress of her job lately.

4

Twenty romantic questions

the only thing you'll need to buy for this gesture is some note cards. But you'll also need to bring to it a couple of things that probably aren't your strong suit: a good memory and a willingness to talk about mushy stuff while keeping a straight face.

She thinks you don't remember anything, just because she remembers *everything*. At least, she remembers every time you screwed up. That time you didn't ask directions and got lost in Petaluma? You'll be reminded of it every time you get ready to take her someplace new. You're above all that silly retribution stuff though, aren't you? You only remember the good stuff. Prove it to her with a romantic version of twenty questions.

For this version, come up with a list of romantic persons, places, or things. For example, one place might be the site of your first date. If a mutual friend introduced you to each other, then he or she might be one of the people. If you once bought her a stuffed animal to make up for saying or doing something egregiously stupid, then it would make a perfect thing.

You can play this game one of two ways, depending on your level of creativity—or patience. One way is to make her do all the work. Write up your list on some note cards and have her ask questions to determine the romantic items. If you really want to impress her, then come up with the clues yourself. For example, let's say you spared no expense on your first date and took her to *Chez* McDonald's. So, you'd offer clues like: You can't have it your way here. I'm filled with special sauce. I'm known for my meat.

Give her a kiss each time she gets the right answer. And be prepared to share intimate memories: the way you made her laugh by sticking French fries up your nose, the way you suavely ordered her Filet o' Fish for her. This may be the hard part for you, but suffer through it. You'll remind her of how you fell in love without having to spend a dime . . . unless you don't have note cards in the house.

This gesture is good for "little" anniversaries, like the anniversary of your first date or the day you got engaged. You're just not likely to get away with an absolutely free romantic gesture on the "big" anniversary.

5

Just married . . . again

for this gesture, you need to be married . . . and you need to get creative. Items can include cans, balloons, streamers, and something you can paint with that's easily removable.

Ah, your wedding day. You were hung over from your bachelor party. You were in a monkey suit for the first time since the prom. You had to remember to say, "I do" at the right times. You wore a plastic grin as you met obscure relatives. On the plus side, you got to enjoy an open bar, dance the funky chicken and the YMCA, and—oh yeah—marry the woman of your dreams and live happily ever after. Admit it: It was one of the best days of your life.

When the reception was over, you went out to your car to find it decorated like Mardi Gras: "Just married," "2-gether 4-ever," "He's just in it for the sex." It was covered in balloons. Tin cans were strung from the bumper. God only knows what else your friends did to your ride. You spent the first few months after your honeymoon getting that damn car back to normal and dreamed of the day you could seek revenge on your bachelor friends.

The clean-up portion sucked, but it was still exciting to see your car decorated like a cheap carnival, right? Bring back that day for both of you by decorating her car the same way: "Just married again," "Still 2-gether 4-ever," "I'm still just in it for the sex." Festoon her ride with balloons and streamers and whatever else your imagination conjures up. This time, though, use something that will clean easily.

This gesture is best for a weekend close to your anniversary, when she isn't likely to need her car. She may not appreciate it if she has to drive to work with her car decked out.

6

Welcome to my world

for this gesture, all you need is the ability to be vulnerable for a short period of time. Really . . . you can do it.

In even the closest relationship, you and she will have different interests. She loves NASCAR. You love petunias. Whatever. Chances are, you've never told her *why* you love the things you do. She's come to accept the wall of dead animal heads in the den or the fact that you bury your nose in a book for hours, seemingly oblivious to the rest of the world—including her. That's the rub. To her, your interests can be a barrier. They're something that separate you from her. Just because she accepts them as part of you doesn't mean she's happy about it.

Amaze and astound her one day by inviting her into your world. You can do this in a straightforward manner, by striking up a conversation about the bizarre crap you love. Be honest. Write stuff down beforehand, if it helps. Or you can introduce her to your twisted little world in a clever way. Pretend you're the host of a new reality show: "The World of Stupid Guy Stuff." This week's episode features you. Take her into your sacred domain and explain to her just why this stupid guy stuff is so important to you.

For instance, the dead animal heads may gross her out. But to you, they're a reminder of some of the best times you ever spent with your dad. He was distant and aloof almost all the time, except when he had a gun in his hand and was aiming it at defenseless animals. If he hugged you after tagging an elk—and that's the only time he ever hugged you—tell her that. You get extra points if you can manage to summon up a tear or two at this memory. You're a bookworm? All she knows is that you give her annoyed looks when she tries to stop you in midparagraph. Bare your soul. Tell her that when you were a kid, you felt your parents were distant and rarely paid attention to you. You learned to find joy through escape into fictional worlds, and to this day, nothing calms you like reading.

Will this "very special episode" of "The World of Stupid Guy Stuff" make her feel any less grossed out by glassy eyes and perpetually bared fangs or all the times you'll make her wait as you explore the nooks and crannies of dusty used book stores? No. But most likely she won't mind them as much as she once did because she understands what they mean to you, the most important man in her life.

This gesture is especially appropriate if your interests have caused an argument. After you've cooled down, put on your pith helmet and take her into the wilds of deepest, darkest you-land.

Just be a kid

items for this gesture are as varied as your imagination. The bad news? You need to devote yourself to a full day with her . . . no slinking into your fortress of solitude.

Remember when you were a kid, and you thought being a grown-up would be so cool? No one could tell you that you couldn't eat marshmallows and pizza for breakfast. You could stay up as late as you want. You could buy whatever you want. No one would be the boss of you! Then, you grew up, and . . . aw crap. It turned out that adulthood just means icky responsibility and bills, bills, bills. And any time you decide to do something stupid and immature because you're an adult now and can get away with it, chances are your conscience prickles your scalp and stops you in your tracks. Damn! They *did* get through to you! Your parents ruined adulthood! Well, give yourself permission on the next federal holiday to act like kids together.

Start off the day with cookies for breakfast, or candy bars, or ice cream—whatever favorite treat you both enjoy. As long as neither of you are alcoholics, don't drink coffee. Tipple Mimosas and a Bloody Mary. Give her a teddy bear or other stuffed animal wearing a sweater with her name or nickname on it. Then take a bubble bath together, surrounded by a bunch of rubber duckies. After that, you might want to, um, jump on the bed.

Play some childhood board games, most of which you can find at your local thrift store. Remember how much fun Chutes and Ladders used to be? There's no law that says adults can't play it. Or Candyland? Or—best of all—Twister. This "harmless" game that bends you into interlocking pretzels is nothing so much as foreplay in a box. Later, break out some Silly Putty and use it to copy pictures or comic strips in the local paper that remind you of one another. Be silly as you talk about these stretchable sentiments of love. Pick up some bubble-blowing solution and cover your living room in bubbles.

If you decide to go out, buy something you don't need, as long as you can afford it. Make hogs of yourselves at your favorite fast food place. Head for the local amusement park and ride the bumper cars or merry-go-round. If you don't have an amusement park, go to something similar. When dinner time rolls around, head to one of those pizza places that's more about video games and animatronic, music-playing-and-singing animals than it is about food. Or go to the local mall's candy store and buy your favorites.

This gesture is great for days off or weekends, especially if your careers are particularly stressful. This can be a great way to get closer to each other and to forget about work for a while.

8

The way to a woman's heart

for this gesture, you'll need to dust off or convincingly fake your culinary skills. You'll need some candles and flowers. You'll also need some preparation time, which can be an unofficial excuse for leaving work early one day. And you might have to overcome your fear of reading instructions.

Food. It isn't just the quickest way to men's hearts anymore. Women appreciate having a favorite meal prepared for them as much as you do. Be her personal chef for an evening. But, but . . . I have trouble following the instructions on the back of TV dinners, you say. I once managed to burn water. It took me months to master the fine art of pouring milk on my Frosted Flakes. Not to worry. You know how, every so often, you have to sneak a peek at an instruction manual in order to maintain your title as Mr. Super-Fix-It? Well, they also make these pretty similar step-by-step instruction manuals called cookbooks. The only difference is that you work with spatulas instead of socket wrenches and you work with food instead of with the items in your toilet tank.

If you're not sure what her favorite meal is, then ask her folks or one of her friends. If you ask her, she'll know something's up. Guys and the subtle extraction of information just don't mix. Once you know what she likes, go to the library and find a cookbook that features that recipe. Or you can probably find the meal online. Go to a search engine and type in Quiche Lorraine or Duck *L'Orange* or Fried Opossum with Niblets or whatever it is she likes. Chances are, several recipes exist in cyberspace.

Once you've got that recipe in hand, follow the instructions. No shortcuts! No additions! If the recipe says "three teaspoons of sugar," don't make the executive decision that ten will be even better. If you stick to the recipe, there's no reason you can't prepare her favorite sumptuous feast as easily as you can put a new ball system in the tank of your porcelain throne. Get the meal ready when she's not home, and surprise her with it. Make sure to set the table with your finest china. If you don't have fine china, use the regular stuff. Just don't use paper plates. Also, create a centerpiece for the table. Buy a floral arrangement, and place it and some candles at the center of the table. Make sure the candles are a scent she likes. You'll totally screw up this gesture if she loathes the odor of vanilla, and that's what you've chosen for the centerpiece. Even if your culinary creation sucks, she'll love it . . . because you made it and made the effort to create a special atmosphere at the dinner table.

And if you already are the cook in the relationship, you can still attempt a variation of this gesture. If you prefer fine French cuisine, for example, and she prefers fine frozen French fries, then humor her and cook her up a mess of whatever dreck she likes to attack with a knife and fork.

This is a good Valentine's Day gesture because it's cheaper than taking her to your city's finest restaurant, and she'll appreciate it just as much as a trip to *Chez Swanke*. But you can perform this gesture anytime.

9

Mr. Sympathy

for this gesture, you need to exude sympathy . . . or at least a good imitation of it.

You know those jars you open for her and those spiders you kill? She appreciates your manliness, really she does. But chances are you don't do such a good job with emotional support. And that's a shame because she loves it when you give her sympathy after she's hurt herself or pulled a muscle—even more than she appreciates your bug-murdering abilities. Admit it. She works harder than you do because women can multi-task. For her, it's all in a day's work to talk on the phone while paying bills and writing a concerto for French horn and orchestra in her head. For guys, multitasking is sitting on the toilet while reading a magazine. This is probably why God made women the childbearers.

So, when she comes in holding her shoulder because the ax was too heavy after chopping the wood or complaining of tennis elbow because of an extra-heavy laundry basket, give her a kiss and tell her how wonderful she is. Tell her you'll give her an hour-long massage at the next commercial break. OK, you don't have to go that far, but at least give her some sympathy instead of a half-assed remark and a thousand-yard stare. Yeah, yeah, you were raised to shrug off pain, to put on your pads and play hurt. If you broke an arm, and the bone stuck out from your body at a ninety-degree angle, *then* you might have cried. Otherwise, you responded stoically to pain. Maybe you think she's being a wimp when she acts like she's dying just because she hit her funny bone. But you don't get it.

Most of the time, she's not really in serious pain, and she knows that. She just wants you to acknowledge the effort she puts into both of your lives every day. She will be amazed when you offer genuine—or genuinely faked—sympathy because you're paying attention to her emotional needs. And hey, if you do this, you'll probably get luckier more often.

This gesture is good for any time it's clear she's feeling underappreciated. For most guys, that means this gesture will be good at any time.

No-tell motel

for this gesture, you'll need to spend a little cash and do a little bit of planning. It will be worth it.

Your home or apartment is your castle, but sometimes it can start to feel like a satellite office: a place besieged by bills, full of phone calls, and crammed with stacks of stuff brought home from your real job. You and she need a vacation, and you don't have to spend a fortune or even go too far away to have one.

Get out a map of your state and look for places that are roughly an hour from your front door. If you live in Middle America or most parts of the South, you probably won't be close to any true vacation paradise, but that's OK. The goal of this gesture is just to get away together, and where you go isn't that important. Once you've targeted a few likely towns, cities, or hamlets, go on the Internet and see if any of these nearby getaways have bed and breakfast inns. Most likely, they will. Once you've found the place you think she'll like, make a reservation. Since the inn is in a town with one stoplight instead of, say, Disneyworld, it's probably going to have vacancies.

After you've booked a room for the weekend, give her a call and tell her that you're whisking her away to paradise. Explain a little bit about your plans, and tell her you won't take no for an answer. She'll probably balk at first, thinking of the money you'll spend. Even though she'd never admit it in a million years—because women are always more practical than men—she really, really wants to go. She needs a break as much as you do, so most likely all you'll have to do to twist her arm is tell her you've already got reservations. Then, when Saturday rolls around, sleep late and hit the road. Oh, and guys, make sure you have directions to the place. You will go a long way toward spoiling this gesture if you don't know exactly how to get to the inn and then go to Defcon Four guy mode and refuse to get directions.

It's amazing how a room at the inn hits your psyche. Once you're there, you feel far away from home and its responsibilities, just by being in a whole new place. Bills won't come to you in the bed and breakfast. Someone else does all the chores. Figuratively, you're a million miles from work. And yet, you are only an hour or so away from your mailbox.

When you do this gesture depends, in part, on your bank account. If you're not exactly a Rockefeller, then plan it for a weekend around your anniversary. You might even try to get away with making it your anniversary present. Or you can do this gesture during the off-season, when rates are cheaper. If money's no object, then this gesture works best when she's not expecting it at all.

11

Yes, I'm paying attention

for this gesture, you'll need a dozen roses and—yes—the ability to pay attention.

She thinks you're never paying attention to her, at least that's what she tells you when you're engrossed in the game or your take-home work or your favorite hobby. You've probably gotten to the point where you don't even try to defend yourself anymore. You're not perfect. There ARE times when you tune her out. But you pay more attention to her than she thinks. Prove it to her in a special way.

Pick a day when she, admittedly, does more around the house than you. On Wednesdays, for example, she pays the week's bills, mops the kitchen floor, does the laundry, mows the grass, *and* manages to work a full eight-hour day at the office. With your astute attention-paying abilities, you've managed to notice that she does all of these things every week.

Buy a dozen roses, and hide one in all of the spots she'll have to hit as she does her share of the housework. When she opens the drawer where you keep the checkbook, let her be greeted by long-stemmed red roses. Place some in the mop bucket, the laundry basket, on the seat of the riding lawnmower, etc. If you can find a way to do it, have roses greet her in her cubicle as well—that would be the master stroke because it shows you've actually gone to some trouble for her. When she finds all these flowers, she'll know that you're paying attention to her hard work and that you appreciate all she does.

This is a good gesture for those times when you think she's feeling unappreciated. How will you know? Don't worry. She'll make sure you're aware of how she's feeling.

12

At your service, Madame

for this gesture, you'll need some flowers, some safety pins, and one of your best quilts. You'll need to be willing to devote a day to her. And if you have a monkey suit, that will help.

If you've been together for a while, chances are you don't open the car door for her anymore. It used to be second nature; now it just feels unnatural. But you can bet she misses that everyday gesture of love and respect. Even if you're not willing to make car-door-opening a daily habit, you can play her chauffeur for a day.

One Saturday or Sunday, get up before her and go out to clean the car, thoroughly, inside and out. Make it spotless. Use two coats of wax. Then take the quilt and pin it to the backseat. The idea is to make the back of the car look much fancier than usual. Once you've got the quilt in place, strew the backseat with flowers. When you're done with all of this, go back in and put on your best suit. If you've got a tuxedo, drag it out of the mothballs and put it on . . . if it still fits. You don't want to spoil this gesture by being unintentionally hilarious in an ill-fitting tux.

When she wakes up, tell her that you are her chauffeur. Say something like, "I am at your service, madame." She'll laugh at the sight of you all dressed up first thing in the morning. Tell her that you've booked a reservation at one of the city's fanciest breakfast places, *Chez* McDonald's, and you would like to transport her there at her earliest convenience. Once she's ready to go, escort her to the car. She'll get misty-eyed at the sight of the "fancy" backseat and all the flowers. Take her to Mickey D's and to any other place she'd like to go . . . no questions asked. Open the door for her to enter and exit. Do it with a flourish: bow, kiss her hand, that sort of thing. Be at her beck and call all day. Don't worry about how silly you will look to other guys. You are manly enough to look like a fool for your lady love! They're just a bunch of jealous losers.

This gesture is good for a weekend near her birthday, or it can be a good one to do on a weekend when you've recently done something extremely stupid and man-like . . . in other words, any time.

13

Dutch treat . . . not!

for this gesture, you'll need a good memory. In fact, for this one, you'd better have a good memory. You could screw the whole thing up if you forget crucial details.

It was the best of days. It was the worst of days. It was a day of sweaty palms, uncertainty, babbling, fumbling attempts at strictly hands-off romance, and perhaps even sheer terror. But it also had something special. It was the acorn that grew a great oak, the spark that ignited a great fire. No, it wasn't your junior prom. It was your first date. Chances are, you pulled out all the stops, trying to prove to her that you were worth her time and attention. You were on your best behavior. You opened doors and pulled out chairs. You belched and adjusted yourself in the bathroom.

And guess what? It worked! You hooked her, baby! But are you still on your best behavior? Probably not. It's a sad fact of life most women have to endure: men don't pull out all the stops once the relationship is established. Sure, you might remember to open the car door for her from time to time. Or you remember to compliment her if she's done something new with her hair. As often as not, however, you don't even notice her hair's different. And it doesn't even cross your mind to open the door for her. And embarrassing bodily functions? Hey, if God wanted you to stifle them, he wouldn't have given them to you in the first place. When you do—or don't do—the things you once didn't/did do, it's not like you're intentionally being a heartless, unaware man. You've just moved on from those early days. But she misses the time when you lavished her with care. Make up for it by re-creating your first date.

This gesture is easy to do if you live in the same spot where the two of you took your first shaky steps together. But even if you've moved to a new state, you can probably come pretty close to re-creating that momentous day. If you were in Manhattan then, and took her to the top of the Empire State Building, it's OK if you're now living in Wichita. It has tall buildings too. Take her to the top of one and stare out a window together. If you lived in Orlando and took her to Disneyworld—but now you live in Greensboro—then take her to the local mini-golf/mini-racing-car franchise. Find the same chain restaurant you took her to on your first date, or one that's very similar.

The key to making this work is not to tell her what you're doing. Just tell her you want to take her out on a date. That alone will probably shock her. Then, as you walk in the steps of your initial rendezvous, she'll start to figure out what you're doing. Get ready … she'll probably well up with emotion. She might cry. It's OK. These are good tears, not of the oops-I-must-have-done-something-dumb-again variety. Another key to the success of this gesture is to do all of those little things you did on that initial night: open doors, pull out chairs, order for her, pay for everything. Who knows, you might even decide to continue doing these little things even after the evening ends. On that first date, you spent most of it worried about whether or not you'd get a kiss or anything more when you took her home. This time, you're almost certain to get lucky.

This gesture is good for the anniversary of your first date, a day on the calendar that you'd BETTER have memorized. But you can do it any time you sense the romance is draining from your relationship.

14

Feed her addictions

for this gesture, you'll need chocolate, and lots of it. A gift card to her favorite store in the mall isn't necessary, but add it if you can.

Women love chocolate. They crave chocolate. They *need* chocolate. Why? It's one of life's great mysteries. Sure, you love the stuff too . . . when it's available. If it isn't, it's no big deal. Women, on the other hand, will crawl across broken glass to get to a Baby Ruth. Women also tend to love shoes and purses . . . more of life's great mysteries. You've got, what, two pairs of shoes, right? One's for work, and one's for everything else. You can't fathom why anyone would need more than two, maybe three, pairs of shoes. And purses? What do women keep in those things anyway? They weigh a ton. You can put everything you need in your wallet and pants pockets. At the end of the day, you take all of that stuff out and put it on your dresser. And it takes up about the same amount of space as the average picture postcard.

One night, make like Santa, and fill her shoes and purses with chocolate . . . all kinds of chocolate. Put in the fancy-schmancy stuff, the common Kisses, the mini-bars, the chocolate coins. If it's economically feasible—and if you feel like it—also put in a conspicuous place a gift card to the shop where she buys most of her purses and shoes. When she wakes up to this chocolate cornucopia, you will likely begin your day with a (ahem) bang.

This gesture's good if you've recently argued about money, and both of you have volunteered to buy less of the stuff you love. If she's managed to restrain her spending for a few weeks, then reward her with this gesture. Don't use it to mask the fact that you haven't been so conscientious with your spending, though. If you try to use it as a smoke screen, it will explode in your face.

Search. Click. Instant (free) romance!

for this gesture, all you need is an Internet connection and the willingness to take a few minutes out of your busy day.

Women love romantic cards, and cards are great because they do all the thinking for you. Instead of sitting around, pondering what to say to her, you can buy a card that puts it all down in black and white with romantic phrasing you couldn't come up with if you sat staring at a blank computer screen for three solid hours. But buying cards can be a challenge. It's embarrassing to stand there in the greeting cards aisle, leafing through the mushiest stuff that can be sandwiched between two covers. Women who see you looking through these cards will probably assume you're buying one because you've done something stupid. Even if you *have* made a dumb-male mistake, you don't want to endure the knowing stares of the fairer sex. Finally, the cost of the nicest romantic cards can seriously cut into your beer money.

Thank God for the Internet. It contains numerous Web sites that offer *free* online greeting cards, including:

www.Hallmark.com
www.BlueMountain.com
www.123greetings.com
www.Birthdayalarm.com
www.Adoringyou.com
www.Romantic-ecards.com
www.1lovecards.com

All you need to do is search these sites for the appropriate (usually free) card: Thinking of You, Just Because, Sorry I Screwed Up Big Time. Peruse the cards at your office computer, so you can send her a card during the day. If your boss peeks into your cubicle, just tell him or her you're working hard on a Very Important Project involving online communication.

Most e-card sites allow you to schedule when your card is sent, and most will allow you to send more than one card. You'll really blow her mind if you manage to send her a different card at the same time each day. If you don't mind spending a teeny tiny amount of cash on the woman of your dreams, then you can customize your e-cards, adding three-dimensional graphics or music. Typically, even the free e-cards give you a chance to personalize your message. Don't get fancy. Stick with something like, "Just thinking of you," "I wanted to send this card just because I love you," or "I'm really, really sorry I screwed up big time. I love you."

This gesture is really good for the work week, whether she works at home or in an office. There she is, dealing with multiple deadlines and wishing she hadn't given up smoking, when all of the sudden, a romantic card from you pops into her e-mail's inbox. You will be her hero.

16

Mr. Fix-It

for this gesture, you might actually have to read directions. It's OK. It doesn't make you any less of a man. You'll also need a good set of tools, cleaning supplies, and at least a little bit of handiness.

You know all those broken-down things around the house and those little mistakes you made that irk her just a tad? You know . . . the closet door you broke when you stumbled into it, the darkened light bulbs in fixtures all over the house, the black spots on the fence caused by overaggressive lawn-mowing. You didn't mean to make a mess or be lax in your light-bulb-changing duties. But "I'll do it tomorrows" have a way of getting piled up until you're dealing with a legion of noticeable fix-it projects. Stop stalling, and fix them up—without her having to nag you about it. She will probably be amazed and wonder if her guy has suddenly been replaced by a clone. Once she realizes it really *is* you—and that you took the initiative to fix stuff she's brought up for weeks (or months, or years)—she will be thrilled.

The black spots on the fence? Grab a bottle of bleach and an industrial-strength sponge, and attack that sucker. The light bulbs? Grab a ladder and get to work. While you're at it, fix those loose cabinet hinges with a screwdriver. Fetch a level, and attach the shelves she's been wanting you to put up. And then, when you come in from working on the car, mowing the lawn, or shoveling snow from the driveway, take off your shoes instead of tracking mud all over the house.

This last part of the gesture will really blow her mind. It's the *coup de grace*, and if you don't do it, you will come perilously close to undoing all the good you've worked so hard to do. Women love it when guys pay attention to details like the equation: dirty shoes + clean carpet = dirty carpet. Why? Because they know it's not part of your genetic makeup. If you *are* noticing details, she'll know it's because you've been influenced by her.

This gesture is good any time. In fact, you ought to try to make it a regular occurrence. She'll feel more appreciated and happier, so she'll nag you less. And she's likely to be in the mood for love more often. It's a win-win situation.

17

Clothe her with love

for this gesture, you'll need a friendly neighborhood boutique, department store, or high-class thrift store ...oh yeah, and some money.

Every woman is addicted to one or more of the following: shoes, purses, or clothing. And, every woman believes men have no taste. One reason for that wildly inaccurate assumption is that you probably aren't that great at picking out clothing, purses, or shoes to add to her collection. Why should you be? You don't carry a purse. You have, at most, three pairs of shoes. And, for you, clothing is function, not fashion. Unfortunately, she is likely to misconstrue your lack of fashion sense. She might believe, for instance, that it means you don't pay enough attention to her (otherwise, you'd know how to shop for her), or that you don't care how much effort she puts into looking good (otherwise, you'd know how to shop for her). Prove your love for her—and your latent fashion sense—by picking her up a new outfit she'll love.

If you're not sure what her taste is, look through her closet. First of all, note her size. God help you if you buy something that's too big for her. In fact, you might want to buy something that's two sizes too small . . . on purpose. Even though she'll have to exchange it, she won't mind. In fact, she'll be walking on air due to your "mistake." Once you know her size, observe what kind of outfits she prefers. Think of this as an exciting anthropological exercise, into the heart of deepest, darkest womanhood.

What does she have? A slew of dresses? Sheer shirts or tank tops? Skirts with belts? Sweaters? What are the dominant colors in her closet? More importantly, what colors do you *not* see in there? If you can't decide on an outfit she'd like, you can't go wrong buying a shirt or blouse in her favorite color. Don't try to be clever and buy her something in a "new" color. Your gesture will sink like a lead balloon. You can also narrow down your choices by observing her the next time she says she has "nothing in her closet." Instead of staring with disbelief at what you think is evidence to the contrary, ask her what she means by that. It will probably turn out that she's got, say, plenty of pants, but she lacks tops to go with them. Or vice versa. Now you know what to buy. Can you imagine how surprised she'll be that you actually cared enough to go out and find her that matching shirt or those matching pants?

A note of caution . . . Most women love to shop. You may think that this gesture will curb her habit. That's a nice fantasy. You aren't likely to take away any shopping time from her with this gesture. Sorry. She'll still have 364 days left in the year to shop on her own to her heart's content. Oh, and one final note of caution. Don't forget to enclose a gift receipt with the outfit you buy her, just in case you really *don't* have any latent fashion sense.

This gesture is good for any time after she's accused you of not paying enough attention to her.

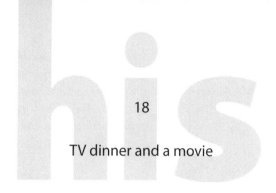

18

TV dinner and a movie

for this gesture, you'll need two TV dinners, a video or DVD, some candles for mood lighting, and a bottle of wine. Two TV-dinner-style fold-up trays are optional.

Although it's not universally true, most men's idea of cooking is Shake 'n Bake or that old favorite, the Hungry Man TV dinner. That doesn't mean you can't turn your weakness into a strength. The next time she calls you at work complaining about not wanting to cook tell her you'll take care of everything. If she balks—thinking of your questionable culinary skills—tell her to trust you. In fact, tell her to consider this gesture an exercise in trust.

Find some excuse to leave work a little bit early—a sick child usually works—even if you don't have one. All you have to do is say it. What boss would argue? On your way home, go by the supermarket and pick up two of your favorite TV dinners, some candles with a scent you know she'll like, and a bottle of wine. Get the good stuff. Stay away from Boone's Farm and Thunderbird, for instance. Pick white Zinfandel. Women seem to love that stuff . . . almost as much as chocolate. If you don't have TV trays, then pick some up. They'll add ambience to this gesture and make it even more special for her.

After the supermarket, head to the local video store. Instead of making a beeline for the new releases, pick up a classic romance. Yes, you will have to rent a chick flick for this gesture. It won't affect your manhood. In fact, it will make you even more macho if you can boldly go up to the clerk with a tearjerker. By the way, if you don't know of any classic romances, ask a store employee. Failing that, *Casablanca* is always a good choice, and it's a film that you might even like.

When you get home, throw the TV dinners into the oven, set up the candles around your TV room, chill that bottle of wine, and pop the movie into your player. Give her a call to find out when she'll probably be home. Ten minutes before she's due to arrive, light the candles. Let the dinners cool on their TV trays. You are ready to be a romantic fool.

This gesture is good for any time, especially when she's been complaining of feeling overwhelmed by household responsibilities.

19

Mr. Mom

for this gesture, you'll need kids—and the courage to do so-called women's work.

Contrary to (your) popular belief, women don't always have to be the primary nurturer and caretaker for your children. Even if—and it's a big if—women are genetically gifted with nurturing genes, that explanation will only work so many times when she asks you to help her out with the kids. Give her the shock of her life by playing mom *and* dad for an entire weekend.

Yes, it might sting a bit to give up the days you usually devote to important pursuits like playing golf, drinking beer, and watching football. But imagine how she'll feel when you wake up at the crack of dawn to feed your baby. Think of how affectionate she'll feel when you give the kids their baths at night, instead of watching *Three Stooges* reruns (again). Give her the chance to soak in the tub or to talk on the phone with her best friend. If you change all the diapers for the day—giving her time to finish baking her favorite chocolate dessert—she will be in the mood for love. And who knows, you may even discover that you *like* spending time with your kids.

This gesture is good for a weekend following one that you spent focusing solely on yourself. When you spent all that time in your own little world, you lost major brownie points. Spending the weekend as Mr. Mom will help you put some capital back into her emotional bank account.

20

Play in the sandbox

for this gesture, you'll need to visit a home-improvement store and buy some sand and a rectangular, deep pan. You'll also need to visit a thrift shop's toy section.

If she sees you paying more attention to your fishing pole or golf clubs than to her, it can make her insecure. You'll know she's feeling that way because she'll start asking you a lot of questions—about your feelings, about your finances, about future plans, about other stuff you don't really want to ponder on the spur of the moment. If you find yourself being constantly peppered with questions, don't get annoyed. What she's really trying to tell you is: Pay attention to ME. What she's really asking is: Do you still love me? Show her that you do by playing in the sandbox . . . grownup style.

Go to a home-improvement or hardware store and buy a bag of sand and a pan into which you'll later pour it. Then go to a thrift store. Thrift stores always have an aisle or two of cast-away toys. Typically, they get so many toys that they bundle up selections of small items, put them into plastic bags, and sell the entire bag for a couple of bucks. Buy several of these bundles. If the store doesn't sell them, then round up a number of loose toys. Don't think too much about it. Just look for different varieties of items, and if you feel pulled to them in some way, pick them up.

When you get home, pour the sand into the pan and spread the toys all over the floor. Try to do it when she's not around, or—even better—perform this gesture in the room of the house that you "escape" into when you want to be alone. Bring her into your fortress of solitude. Tell her you know you've been distracted lately and haven't been paying enough attention to her. Say something like, "To make up for it, I thought we could play in the sandbox for a while." She'll look puzzled, so quickly sit down and show her what you mean.

Pick up one of the toys, put it into the sandbox, and tell her how it reminds you of her. For example, one of the objects is a toy fireplace taken from a doll-house. Put the fireplace in the sand and tell her, "This makes me think of you because you are the warmth of our home." You might pick up a toy boulder, put it into the box, and tell her: "This reminds me of you because you're my rock. You give me strength." If she's not melting by this time, then that rock can symbolize her heart because it must be made of stone. Continue this gesture until you've filled the sandbox. Then let her play. You might be surprised what objects make her think of you. You don't need the sandbox, but it will help put you into a childlike frame of mind that spurs the sort of creativity necessary to pull of this gesture successfully.

This gesture is good for times when you're feeling distant from each other. Keep the sandbox and toys, and bring them out whenever you feel you're not connecting.

21

Say it with music

for this gesture you'll need a recordable compact
disc and a way to burn songs onto it, or you'll need
an old-fashioned cassette and recordable tape player.
You'll also need stacks of your favorite tunes.

The great philosopher Sting once said, "Poets,
priests, and politicians have words to thank for their
positions." But for most men, words are more like stum-
bling blocks than building blocks. She asks you, "Why
do you love me?" And all you can do is stand there
tongue-tied. You know you love her, but it's hard to put
it into words when you're on the spot. The result? You
say nothing or you say something stupid, and either
way you wind up with a one-way trip to Doghouse
Junction. It seems unfair, but you've got to remember
that women are verbal. You, a guy, probably aren't. You
can spend a whole afternoon with your friends, without one of you ever uttering a complete sentence. You

may not have a way with words, but you know how to record your tunes, right? The next time she asks, "Why do you love me?" Answer her with music.

Find songs that make you think of her. Maybe there's one featuring her name, or one that you consider "your" song. Don't be afraid to pick mushy tunes you would never ordinarily admit to liking . . . those songs you tell your friends "ruin" your favorite albums. If you're really a gadget whiz, you can add an introduction to each song: "This song makes me think of you because . . ." If you don't have a way to add these introductions, then recite them for her before you play each song. If you're afraid you'll forget what to say, write yourself a script. Before you play your tape or compact disc, level with her. Tell her you wish you *could* tell her why you love her so much, but since you don't have a way with words, you've made something that you hope will answer for you. Then push "Play."

As noted, this is a good gesture to have ready the next time she asks you that frightening question: Why do you love me? Sooner or later, all women ask it . . . so be prepared.

22

For a good time, call

for this gesture, you'll need an erasable pen, a camera, a photo album . . . and make sure she's got a sense of humor.

Remember junior high school? Love was so simple. All you had to do was write a note that said something like, "I like you. Do you like me? Please check one box." If she put a check in the "yes" box, you were home free. It was off to French kiss central and later, the locker room, where you could try to convince your buddies you'd gone all the way. To prove your love, all you had to do was write her name on the wall of men's bathrooms all over town. Shakespeare and Elizabeth Barrett Browning could keep their sonnets. You immortalized her on the wall of Jimmie's Pump 'n Pee. Not just any girl could claim that. As you get older, love gets more complicated. But if she has a sense of humor, you can relive those golden days of yore with a gesture that's sure to make her laugh—and to show her you went to some trouble for her—always the key to any romantic gesture.

Get an erasable pen and a camera, preferably an instant camera. Then go to as many men's rooms you can find. Write her name on the wall. Add a corny saying or wrap her name in a giant heart, take a picture, then erase all traces of your handiwork. Don't worry. She won't have any trouble figuring out where you took the photos. Even the swankiest men's room still looks like a men's room. Once you assemble all your pictures, put them in a photo album. Give the album to her and say something like, "We didn't know each other then. But I wanted to prove my love to you the same way I did in junior high, when love was simple and holding hands was bliss." She'll never look at Jimmie's Pump 'n Pee the same way again.

This gesture makes a good, romantic gag gift for anniversaries or birthdays. Just make sure you get her a "real" gift as well, or—regardless of her sense of humor—she won't enjoy this gesture.

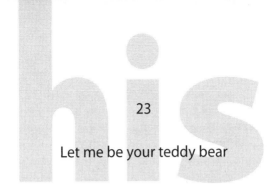

23

Let me be your teddy bear

for this gesture, you need a blank card, your lovin' arms, and patience.

Elvis got it right when he sang about being his love's teddy bear. Why? Because women love to cuddle. Admit it. You think the only equation that makes sense is: cuddling = foreplay. But for women, cuddling is encoded in their DNA. For some reason, men lack this cuddling gene. But that's no excuse. Cuddling makes her feel safe and comforted and proves to her that you can hold her closely without it being a prelude to sex. Defy your genetics and be her teddy bear for the day.

The night before you perform this gesture, get a blank card and write in it something like, "Let me be your teddy bear for the day." Or, instead of a card, turn an index card into a coupon for "Cuddling on demand. Valid one day only." And then commit yourself to a day of sexless intimacy. It will be fun . . . really! No matter what you're doing—watching television, puttering around in the garage, starting your day with Mimosas—drop it whenever she wants to cuddle. Then cuddle for as long as she wants. Let *her* pull away. Don't *you* pull away. You need at least to pretend to enjoy this activity, or this gesture will fail miserably. Who knows? You may even decide you agree with the King of Rock 'n' Roll. It's great to be her lovin' teddy bear.

This gesture is good for those times when it finally dawns on you that she's feeling second best in your life. It will go a long way toward rebuilding or strengthening your relationship.

24

Now starring . . .

for this gesture, you'll need to make arrangements to use the marquee of one or more sympathetic local businesses. It might cost you a few bucks. You also should have a camera.

She probably feels you don't say those three little words nearly enough. Or she thinks you're not public enough in your professions of love. Admit it. When she calls you at work and says, "I love you," you just say, "Thanks honey. I'll see you later." Right? What if somebody hears you and actually believes you love your wife, girlfriend, or fiancée? Your reputation would surely suffer. Reality check. You *do* love her, and it takes a strong man to admit that in front of others. Heck, you ought to announce it to the entire town. She's always dreamed of having her name in lights, right? You can make her lifelong dream come true—and make a very public declaration of your love for her—with this gesture.

Many businesses in your town have marquees to advertise their specials or upcoming events. Call on a few and see if the owners would be willing to let you use their marquee for one day, to advertise your love for her. Some places will probably give you the brush-off, but you're likely to find at least a few businesses willing to let you make a to-order sign for a few bucks. Community theaters are almost always strapped for cash, for instance. If one is between productions, the theater manager will probably be happy to accommodate your request for a small, tax-deductible donation. If your pockets are deep enough, rent a few marquees in different parts of town. Use the establishment's big, plastic letters to spell out simple statements of affection. Or, if you've managed to rent several marquees, have them make one long statement, if read in the proper order.

Once your messages are in place, tell her you're going to take her for a drive. Then go by your marquee or marquees. Make sure she sees it or them. Then, get out of the car and take a picture of her in front of your professions of love. This gesture is sure to make her feel like a star, the star at the center of your galaxy.

This gesture is especially good after you've done something that's landed you in the doghouse (again).

25

Mirror, mirror on the wall

for this gesture, you need dry-erase markers, old eyeliner makeup pencils, and a copy of Shakespeare's sonnets.

Don't try to understand why she spends so much time in front of the mirror. It's in her genes. So is the ability to discern the difference between how she looks with and without makeup. You think she look just as beautiful before and after, right? But when you tell her that, she gets insulted and slams the door on you. You're really trying to tell her that you think she's beautiful no matter what, but somehow, she misunderstands your compliment. There's another way to make the same compliment in a way she'll find acceptable, and all you need is an erasable marker or eyebrow pencil she's discarded.

Before she gets up one morning, write lines from Shakespeare's sonnets on the bathroom mirror in erasable marker or eyebrow pencil. Make sure it's one she doesn't use, or this gesture will be wasted, as she yells at your for breaking her only eyebrow pencil. Why Shakespeare? Because women *love* him. At least, they love it when the men in their lives quote the Bard. It melts the heart of the stoniest damsel. You can find Shakespeare's sonnets on the Internet, at the library, or in a multitude of inexpensive editions.

Or, you can cheat and pick from these:

"How would, I say, mine eyes be blessed made
By looking on thee in the living day."
                                    —Sonnet forty-three

"When that mine eye is famish'd for a look,
Or heart in love with sighs himself doth smother,
With my love's picture then my eye doth feast."
                                    —Sonnet forty-seven

"Sometime all full with feasting on your sight,
And by and by clean starved for a look;
Possessing or pursuing no delight
Save what is had, or must from you be took."
                                    —Sonnet seventy-five

Or, the perfect sentiment:

"I never saw that you did painting need,
And therefore to your fair no painting set."
—Sonnet eighty-three

This gesture is especially good when you've said something stupid about her looks, such as: You're so beautiful. You don't *need* makeup. You think it's a compliment. She thinks it's an insult. No matter how deeply you're in the doghouse, the sight of Shakespeare's sonnets on the mirror will extract you.

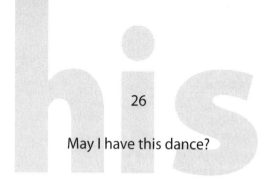

26

May I have this dance?

for this gesture, you'll need to take dance lessons, which means you'll have to (gulp) follow directions to the letter.

If you're like most men, you've danced, perhaps three times in your life: at your junior prom, at your senior prom, and at your wedding. It would be fine with you if you never cut another rug. But women love dancing, almost as much as cuddling. Even if she never says it, she wishes you would again sweep her off her feet and float her around the dance floor, preferably to the song that was the backdrop for the first dance at your wedding reception. You've got two left feet? Don't worry about it. That's what dance lessons are for.

Get out the phone book and look up "dancing instruction." If you're interested only in learning "your" song—and not the meringue, the cha cha, or the Mashed Potato—then make some calls and find a place that will allow you to tailor your instruction. There's no sense in paying for more information than you need. Then take your happy feet to the dance studio, and *follow directions*. Don't be afraid to feel silly. It's much better to make a fool of yourself in front of a stranger you're paying than to do it in front of your significant other in a public place with lots of people watching.

Once you've become a Fred Astaire facsimile—at least on "your" song—then cue it up on your stereo one evening before she comes home from work. As soon as she walks in the door and puts down all of her stuff, ask her the magic question she's been waiting for: "May I have this dance?" Then press "Play" and sweep her off her feet. Another, braver, option is to do this publicly. Take her to a club, pay the disc jockey, and surprise her with a spin around the dance floor. If the thought of countless pairs of eyes trained on you makes your blood run cold and your two feet turn left, then doing this gesture at home is just fine.

This gesture is good for her birthday. It will mean almost as much to her as a two-carat diamond ring . . . almost.

27

Hometown vacation

for this gesture, you'll need to contact your town's visitors' bureau. Caution: You may have to get driving directions.

Vacations are costly endeavors. If you go to a theme park, you pay exorbitant rates for parking, admission, eating, souvenirs, and—probably some-day—breathing the air. And travel? Fuhgeddaboudit! It won't be long before you have to take out a sec-ond mortgage just to fill up your gas tank. Vacations aren't just costly, they're exhausting. Drive time and jet lag can zap the fun out of almost any trip. Unless you decide to be a tourist in your hometown, that is.

Whether you live in Las Vegas or Lewes, Dela-ware, chances are there are a number of museums and cultural attractions in your backyard that you've never considered visiting or attending. The two of you are too busy making a living day-to-day to think of your town as a vacation Mecca. Give your local visitors bureau a call or visit, and you'll probably be surprised to learn all that there is to do, right in your backyard: The Snake-Handler Hall of Fame, The World's Biggest Mud Pie, the graves of obscure Civil War generals, the Museum of Modern American Retro Art. Maybe there's even a winery in your area. The list is endless. Who knows what unexplored treasures exist just across town?

One Saturday, plan a trip to these local tourist traps. Tell her you're going to take her on a fun-filled, exhaustion-free vacation. Let the stops be a surprise, but try to tailor them to her likes. If she's an art lover, visit galleries you never knew existed. If she's a history buff, take her to the site of local Revolutionary War battles. She likes architecture? No problem. Any town or hamlet worth its salt has at least a few ornate, historic homes open to the public. When it's time to eat, take her to a locally famous restaurant you've never visited, like Big Ed's Chicken Pit. You'll spend a fun-filled day together, probably learn something new about each other, and you might even start to appreciate where you live.

This gesture is great for a Saturday when she complains about how there's "nothing to do." Tell her, "Oh, yeah? We'll just see about that." And hit the road.

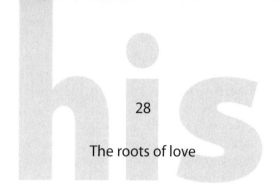

28

The roots of love

for this gesture, you'll need to visit a nursery and buy a tree. You'll also need to have a shovel and be prepared to do some heavy-duty digging.

Trees are living, breathing symbols of romance. You kissed her for the first time in the shade of a mighty oak. You made love, hidden under the cascading limbs of a weeping willow. You've had countless picnics amid the heady scent of pines and firs. In addition to shared memories, trees are also romantic because of the many ways you can compare them to your love for her: planted firmly, growing steadily, enduring for the ages, forming the very air that you breathe. So, what could be more romantic than planting a tree in honor of your relationship?

Go to a nursery and tell the proprietor what you plan to do. She'll help you find the right kind of tree—namely, one that's easy to care for. This gesture won't pack much punch if the damn tree dies before sprouting its first leaves. When you get home, find the right spot to plant your tree, and dig the hole for it. Try to do it when she's not there, or when she's otherwise occupied indoors. When you've prepared the site, tell her what you plan to do and why you want to do it. Play up all that stuff about how the tree reminds you of her because it provides the air you breathe and how it will last for centuries, just like your love. Say this with a straight face and in a solemn tone. Make a whole ceremony out of this gesture. In no time, she'll be planted on your lips and rooted deeply in your warm embrace.

This gesture is good for the springtime. It's a good one for getting you out of the doghouse as well.

29

Your future scrapbook

for this gesture, you'll need to gather pictures from magazines or other sources and put them into a scrapbook.

No matter how confident she is, there are times when she wonders just how committed to her you are. She frets about the future, wondering if you consider her a part of it. She probably has a scrapbook to serve as a roadmap of your past. Do her one better. Reassure her about the times ahead by creating a scrapbook of your future together.

Gather a stack of old magazines and look for pictures that you hope will represent that future. For example, if all you've got right now is a roach-infested apartment with a view of garbage cans, cut out a photo of a massive mansion. Or be realistic, and just make it a photo of a nice, three-bedroom/two-bath home surrounded by a white picket fence. You're sharing a 1978 Buick Regal with a rattletrap muffler? Create a rosier future, filled with Jaguars, BMWs, and a shiny black Mercedes-Benz. Vacations are a mere fantasy? Cut out photos of the Himalayas, Tahitian beaches, or Sun Valley ski slopes to represent carefree days to come. Make sure you add at least a few photos of happy, older couples, to symbolize your lasting commitment to her.

Once you've gathered a nice crop of future photos, put them in a scrapbook. Write captions for the photos, such as, "Here's the house we'll share someday" and "This is the car I'll buy you one day." Label the front cover of the scrapbook, "Our Future Together." Then, the next time you sense she's doubtful of your commitment, bring out the book you've made.

This gesture is good for Valentine's Day or any time she doubts your commitment. Yes, you'll know.

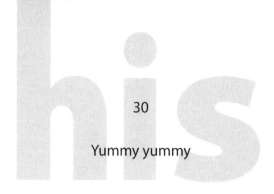

30

Yummy yummy

items you need for this gesture are: Lollipops, red ribbon, some preplanning.

When she was little and got sick and her mom took her to the doctor, a lollipop afterward just seemed to make things all better. To this day, she will respond to the healing and loving effect of lollipops. Don't be a sucker. Indulge her with a slew of these tasty treats the next time she recovers from a temporary illness or the next time she seems depressed about something. Yes, you'll know.

Go bananas. Lollipops come in all shapes and sizes. Some whistle. She can wear some on her finger. Some even taste like tequila and have worms in them, but you're better off skipping those and giving them to friends at bachelor parties in hopes that they'll puke on camera. Locate one of those old-fashioned candy emporiums that sell giant drums of candy and those big, swirly lollipops that evoke days of old spent in little houses on the prairie. Buy a bunch of lollipops in various shapes, sizes, and flavors. On your way home, pick up some red ribbon and tie it around your lollipop bouquet. Hide this treat somewhere she'll never look—in your sock drawer, for instance.

Now, the evening's ready. When she's feeling better, take her out to her favorite restaurant and to see a movie she'll like—something without car chases and huge explosions, something with tons of huggin' and kissin'. Afterward, take her to that candy shop. Let her pick out some favorites. Tell her something like, "I wanted to take you to a place that's almost as sweet as you." This gesture will fail miserably if you cannot say this with a straight face. She'll love it. When you return home, tell her to close her eyes and wait for a big surprise. Then get out your lollipop bouquet and leave it on her pillow. She'll be amazed that you actually planned ahead for this gesture, and it will remind her of the sweet evening you've spent together. She won't call you a thoughtless creep again . . . until you do something that's off-the-charts stupid.

This gesture is good for a time when she's been sick or just down in the dumps.

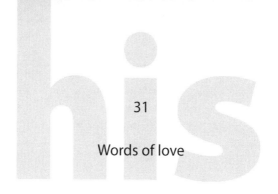

31

Words of love

for this gesture, you'll need stacks of old magazines, poster board, scissors, and some glue.

You wish you were a silver-tongued devil, able to spew out romantic expressions like a stock ticker spews out results of the latest quarterly reports. It would make life so much easier if only you had the right words at the right time. Sure, you can buy a card. There's nothing wrong with that. But it's someone else's soul-baring sentiments. Wouldn't you like—just once—for the words to be those you've chosen? Done. Get a stack of old magazines filled with advertising copy in large print, and you've got an instant word salad from which to fashion your own words of love.

First, put her name at the top of a large piece of poster board. Leave plenty of blank space underneath. Then comb the ads for words that make you think of her. Does she comfort you when you're feeling concerned about your job? Look for a Southern Comfort ad, and clip away. Is she your best friend? Search until you find those words. Is she fun? You'll be hard-pressed to find an ad that *doesn't* have that word in it somewhere. Keep looking and clipping: "lover," "beautiful," "special," "thoughtful." Fill up the piece of poster board, but leave some room at the bottom. There, in your own writing, add the words: I LOVE YOU.

This gesture is good for when she needs to be reminded of how you feel about her. The great thing about this gesture is that she'll be able to hold onto it and be reminded of how you feel during your tongue-tied times.

32

Warm and fuzzy

for this gesture, you'll need to purchase a variety of warm, fuzzy items, so plan this for a birthday or anniversary.

Ah, women. Whether she's a tomboy or a modern princess, a Wall Street shark or the very embodiment of Mother Earth, she's soft and warm. And chances are, she likes to be surrounded by all things warm and fuzzy. Make her wish your command.

The next time her birthday rolls around, scour the earth—or at least the local mall—and load up on the softest items you can find on the shelves. Comb stores' collections of cashmere. Find some fuzzy bunny slippers. Angle for an angora sweater. Go from shop to shop until you find the softest blanket made by human hands. Don't stop there. Slip her into slipper socks. Cap her in a warm, fuzzy—but very chic—chapeau. Once you've rounded up as many different items as you can find (and afford), take them home, hide them, and wait for her big day. She'll love you for pampering her with the softest, fuzziest items you can find—and for being manly enough to buy them in the first place.

This gesture will set you back a few bucks, so do it only on a special occasion.

33

If I had a million dollars

for this gesture, you'll need a large greeting card, glue, and pictures of what you'd buy her, if you had a million dollars.

Someday you'll hit the lottery or be the guy who calls the shots. Until then, you're lucky if you have enough to buy her gifts that don't come from a gumball machine. Don't worry. She knew you weren't a Rockefeller when the relationship began. She loves you for you. And it's the thought that counts, right? The next time you give her the gift you can afford, add a card filled with images of what you'd get her if you were loaded with cash.

If you're a soon-to-be-discovered artist, you can draw these fantasy gifts. But if you have trouble tracing stick figures, that's OK. If you've got a mailbox, you probably get catalogues that wind up in a pile somewhere before they're thrown away. Look through these for appropriate pictures. Or flip through magazines. Don't just find expensive stuff. Find expensive stuff she'll really like. If the sight of open water makes her go into hysterics, then don't cut out a picture of a yacht. But if she loves jewelry and has nothing but costume pieces, find photos of the fanciest brooches, bracelets, baubles, and bangles you can find. Make sure the pictures are small enough for you to be able to glue them into the card. When you're done, write something like this under the card's message: "If I had a million dollars, I'd buy all of this and more for you." Unless she has a heart of stone, she'll melt at this gesture.

This gesture is good for a gift-giving occasion.

34

Romantic coupons

for this gesture, you'll need index cards and a pen or marker.

Most women love to shop, so most of them love coupons. Consider those flyers that come in the mail . . . you know the ones. They promise an extra 15 percent off any regular priced item in the store if the "shopper of the house" acts within three days. To you, these cards are junk mail. Or worse, you think they're manipulative propaganda, designed to get her to spend money she otherwise might have saved—or spent on you! Don't get mad. Get even. Make up some romantic coupons that won't send her skipping down the road to the nearest boutique . . . which, you know, is French for "obscenely overpriced stuff no one really needs."

If you're artistic, make each coupon a little work of art. If you're not, that's OK. You can keep them simple instead. The idea here is to think of all the things that you know she likes for you to do . . . and that you rarely do. Consider these examples: One free, ten-minute backrub. One thorough tub cleaning, without whining or complaining. One free, homecooked dinner not made by you. Foreplay for more than five minutes. Be a gentleman, and put in a coupon that lets her go shopping without you nagging her about money. And finally, you might try to slip in—for yourself—a "get out of the doghouse free" card.

These coupons make great stocking stuffers or secondary Valentine's Day presents. Yes, "secondary." Don't try to get away with giving her only these coupons, unless you want your gesture completely ignored.

35

Burma-Shave

for this gesture, you'll need to make a series of signs
that you stick into the ground. Wooden stakes, card-
board, and a staple gun should do the trick.

Once upon a time, Burma-Shave signs were the
poetry of the American roadside. The product itself
was just shaving cream, but the company advertised
it with an immortal campaign. Instead of individual
billboards, Burma-Shave ads featured a series of six
signs, which—when read in order—formed a rhym-
ing jingle. The last sign drivers passed always bore the
name of the product. From the 1920s through the
mid-1960s, Burma-Shave signs dominated the land-
scape. With this gesture, you can shamelessly steal the
Burma-Vita company's idea, and make her smile at the
start of your next road trip.

Vacations that start with long drives don't always
have the best of beginnings. You're in the car with

each other for hours. You don't share the same taste in music, so there's a continuous fight over the car stereo. She hates to drive, but she complains the entire time you're behind the wheel. One of the main reasons these drives are often Purgatory on wheels is because you're both stressed and focused solely on all the miles of blacktop ribbon looming ahead of you. You can take your minds off of the trip ahead by making up a series of signs and planting them along the road the day before you sally forth. Be clever and romantic. Most of the old Burma-Shave advertisements used six signs, but you can use as many as you like. Here are some suggestions:

Sign one: YOU'RE THE GIRL
Sign two: I'LL FORGET NEVER
Sign three: I HOPE THAT WE'RE
Sign four: TOGETHER FOREVER

Sign one: WHILE ON THE ROAD
Sign two: YOUR TORCH I CARRY
Sign three: YOU'RE THE GIRL
Sign four: I'M GLAD I MARRIED

Sign one: WHILE ON VACATION
Sign two: LET'S TAKE A CHANCE

Sign three: AND PRACTICE MUCH
Sign four: SOME SWEET ROMANCE

Tailor the signs by making jingles that rhyme her name with other words. And be a good citizen by removing the signs when you return from your trip. She'll be impressed that you went to the trouble to set up this gesture just before a long trip, and you'll be able to avoid any wholesale nagging for at least a few rest area visits.

This gesture is good for your next summer vacation or weekend getaway.

36

Tie a red ribbon 'round the ol' oak tree

for this gesture, you'll need tons of red ribbon and a pair of scissors.

If you're smart, you give her flowers and candy on a somewhat regular basis, and not just: (1) on her birthday, (2) on Valentine's Day, or (3) when you've done something really, really dumb and thoughtless. She loves these "just because" flowers because they mean you're thinking about her at times other than special occasions and days when you're in the doghouse. But the next time you want to use flowers to tell her how much you love her, consider decorating the trees in your yard instead.

Flowers die. Chocolates make her fat. Besides, those gifts are a cliché, and you're a unique kind of guy, right? Go to a craft store and buy at least a hundred yards of red ribbon. Hide it in the trunk of your car. The next time she's away for several hours, cut the ribbon into lengths long enough to tie around the trees in your yard. Attack this gesture with gusto. Be manly. Get out a ladder and tie the ribbons high. Tie some ribbons low. Tie them in-between. Turn your oaks and birches into beacons of love. When you're done, give her a call on her cellular phone. Tell her to expect a romantic surprise when she gets home.

This is a good "just because" gesture that can replace giving flowers and candy.

37

A cultural evening

for this gesture, you'll need to dress up and endure an evening of cultural pursuits. You must at least pretend to enjoy this, for her sake. You'll probably need to visit your local library. You'll need to pick up something fancy for dinner, and you may need to pick up a bottle of wine and some candles.

It's not universally true, but most guys wouldn't know culture if they found it in a petri dish. And while some women can rattle off stats and personnel changes within every collegiate athletics conference, most prefer the finer arts: ballet, opera, classical concertos, Greek drama. You've had to feign illnesses and "emergency meetings" at work more times than you can count in order to get out of an evening in uncomfortable clothes spent listening to big-boned men and women warble in . . . what is that . . . German? Italian? Pig Latin? But there are times when the gods of romance need a sacrifice. And your time has come. This weekend, exchange pass rushing with *pas de bourree*.

Give her an evening of cultural entertainment at home. Ask a female colleague or your local arts council for help. First, find a way to get her out of the house for a while so you can set up the evening. Your local library is likely to have videos of classic ballets and operas. Find one that's to your liking by reading a synopsis of the video box. Most operas are total downers, but you need to stick with one that details love denied, rather than say, a man murdering his lover. And ballet? Heck, it's people in tights on their tiptoes, turning in circles. Just grab a tape. While you're at the library, you should also pick up some music, if she doesn't already have a trove of classical recordings at home. Stick with the greats: Mozart, Beethoven, Mendelssohn. Pick up an Italian dish on the way home. Not pizza . . . something fancy. Snag a bottle of fine wine. That's the stuff that comes with a cork, not a twist-off cap. When you return home, put on your best suit. Light some candles. Put classical music on the stereo. When you hear her coming to the door, open it and say something like, "Your presence is requested at an evening of cultural entertainment. Please come in, Madame." Then take her to the table, which you will have covered with a tablecloth and set with your finest china. By now, her head should be spinning. And when you tell her that the next item on the program is a private viewing of a ballet or opera, she'll freeze midfork. If you're really lucky, she'll be so overcome by passion at the thought of your sacrifice that she'll immediately take you to the bedroom, and you won't have to watch the ballet after all. But if you do have to watch, make a show of enjoying it. Or at least ask her a lot of questions, so that she can feel she's actually enlightening you.

This gesture is good after you've dragged her to sporting events or hogged the television one too many times. It might be a sacrifice for you, but you might actually learn something. Oh, and by the way, a *pas de bourree* is that ballet move where the ballerina runs around on her tiptoes. If you can use it in a sentence during the evening, you will definitely get lucky.

38

Setting the house aglow

for this gesture, you'll need to find items that glow in the dark. Items should range from rubber duckies to glow sticks to glow-in-the-dark necklaces.

Women love romantic mood lighting, probably because it accompanies every love scene from every film ever made in Tinseltown. A couple in a movie could have a tryst on the surface of the sun, and somehow the director would contrive to create shadows and a cosmic dimmer switch. Maybe you've already tried the candle route—a good choice. But if you want to create that same kind of magical illumination in a more unique way, go for the glow.

The next time you go catch a basketball game, pick up handfuls of those glow sticks vendors sell for the kids in the stands. Go to a novelty store and pick up other glowing items. You'll probably be able to find enough to simulate daylight: necklaces, plastic statues, and even rubber duckies. The ducks are a must. You may have to search online for them. Once you've rounded up an assortment of glowing products, wait for an evening that she works late. Then set the house aglow. Finish by preparing her a relaxing bath complete with, you guessed it, glow-in-the-dark duckies. When you're done, turn off all the lights in the house and wait for her arrival. When she gets home, be sure you're sitting on the couch acting like nothing is unusual. When she makes a mention of the glowing items, you can say something cheesy like, "What glowing items? It must be you who's lighting up this room with the passion you feel for me." Hopefully, she's had a good day, and this line will work. Otherwise, cut your losses and show her the tub. After she's soaked amid the ducks, her passion may indeed start to smolder.

This is a good "just because" gift, or you can use it as the prelude to her birthday.

39

A bun in the oven

for this gesture, she needs to be pregnant for the first time. As for you, you'll need: shoes that are too small for you, socks that are too tight on your ankles, a pillow, string, a 20-pound book . . . as well as patience, gusto, courage, vulnerability, love, and understanding.

Your contribution to the miracle of birth was easy. Heck, it was fun! She's got it a little more difficult. And no matter how sympathetic and helpful you are, you don't really know what it's like for your hormones to go crazy and to put on 50 pounds or more, without touching a bottle of malt liquor. And you're likely to get annoyed from time to time. For example, she'll put on so much weight so quickly, that she'll snore loudly through the night. She'll take up most of the bed without even trying. You'll have to tie her shoes for her when she can't bend over to do this task herself. Before you roll your eyes or berate her for interrupting your sleep, try this gesture. She's got to be pregnant for nine months. See if you can survive having a bun in the oven for just twenty-four hours.

On your next day off, stick a heavy book or two in a pillowcase and tie the case around your waist. Put on too-tight socks and too-small shoes. Don't get near caffeine or alcohol. Now, go about your business. Experiment with the joy of getting into and out of a car. Thrill to how much fun household chores become. And finally, enjoy the difficulties of sleep. You either have to sleep on your left side or with your upper body propped up on pillows. Fun, huh? The next day, compare notes with her. Chances are, you'll appreciate what she's going through a lot more. And you'll learn just how strong a person she is. And while twenty-four hours isn't exactly nine months, she'll appreciate that you attacked this gesture with gusto and managed to survive an entire day as a pregnant man.

This gesture is good when she's several months pregnant and you've found yourself feeling less than sympathetic about her condition.

40

Playing in the snow

for this gesture, you'll need a heavy snowfall, a shovel, a childlike spirit, and some elbow grease.

Aw crap, it snowed last night. Thank God it's Saturday, so you don't have to worry about chipping the cars out of their suits of ice in order to get to work and be yelled at by the boss for being a little late. But it's still a pain. Winter wonderland, my ass. Hey, wait a minute! Remember? Once upon a time you loved snow. It was like a "get out of jail free" card in Monopoly. You could spend hours building snow forts, having snowball fights, sledding backward down the scariest hills to prove your mettle. Those carefree days are behind you, but you can bring them back a bit with this gesture. And you can show her that you love her in the process. What a deal!

The next time Jack Frost takes a dump all over your front lawn, first be industrious. Break out the snow shovel, and clear a path down the sidewalk to the car, just in case she needs to go somewhere. That's the no-fun part of this gesture. Once that's over, use the shovel to clear out trenches in the snow that spell out I ♥ U. Then surround your message with a legion of snow angels. That's the loving part of the gesture. Finally, go to it. Build a couple of heavy-duty snow forts, one on either side of the lawn. Then make up a batch of first-rate snowballs to store behind each fort. When you're done with all of this, go inside, make some coffee or tea, and serve her some. Then tell her you've got a wintry surprise in store. Go out, throw snowballs. Make a snowman. Then go back in and have some hot chocolate—or warm each other up in any way you'd like.

This gesture is good for a snowy, blustery day.

Flattery will get you everywhere

for this gesture, you need to be observant, and you need to practice sincere flattery.

Admit it. She could wear a brand new outfit while sporting a fresh hairstyle and you probably wouldn't notice. You might realize something's different, but you won't be able to put your finger on it. Worse . . . you might make the mistake of asking a truly dangerous question like, "Have you lost weight?"

As a species, guys just aren't that observant. To you, she looks the same before and after she sits in front of her makeup mirror. But women tend to notice small details. It's one of the things that make them special. You forget to send a card to your brother, while she knows the birthdays and addresses of distant cousins and friends she hasn't seen in a decade. But being born without detail-oriented genes is no excuse for your faulty powers of observation. She takes a lot of pride in her appearance, and she expects you to—no, demands that you—notice when she's tried something new.

The best way to build your perceptive strength is to compliment her on something new each day. But the trick is: You must be sincere in your flattery. If she's got bed-head, don't compliment her on her hair. If she's wearing an "I'm with Stupid" sweatshirt and splotchy, stained sweatpants, don't tell her you really love her outfit. Check out her nails. Did she just have them done? Has she had highlights added to her hair? Pay attention to the colors of lipstick and eye shadow she uses, so you can detect any changes. Look closely . . . you'll find something.

Once you do, don't slather on the flattery with a trowel. But do make it clear to her that you're paying attention to her. Say something like, "I just noticed that you had your eyebrows waxed. They look great." Or, "I see you've had highlights added to your hair. They're really flattering." Make sure you say these things with a straight face and a sincere tone. Don't be afraid of appearing unmanly because you're noticing eyebrow waxings and rouge shades. There's nothing manlier than making her feel great about herself. Sincere flattery will indeed get you everywhere.

This gesture is one you should begin immediately.

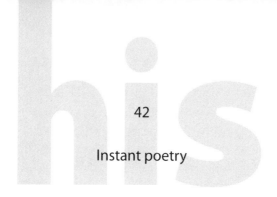

for this gesture, you'll need a large sheet of poster board, scissors, and a permanent marker.

You're not a poet, and you know it. You wouldn't know a trope if it alliterated all over you. And the only poem you have committed to memory begins, "There once was a man from Nantucket." No problem. With this gesture, you can make instant poems for her anytime, and leave them in places where she's sure to notice them.

Cut a large piece of poster board into small rectangles. Make the smaller pieces large enough to write words on with a permanent marker. On the rectangles write the following words: love, is, are, you, your, to, too, sun, my, warmth, joy, beauty, special, unique, sweet, vivacious, extraordinary, sensual, sexy, super, funny, smart, heart, adorable, as, the, promise, pledge, committed, feelings, emotions, powerful, lovely, red, blue. Don't stop there. Add any other words that come to mind when you think about her . . . when you're thinking kindly of her. And write her name on several pieces of poster board, of course.

Once you have all of these words, arrange them into simple poetic statements. For example, "Your love is joy to my heart" or "You are unique as the sun." Leave these sentiments in places where she's sure to see them. Put one on the bathroom sink first thing in the morning, before she's up. Put another on the kitchen table. Leave her a poem on the seat of her car. She'll love you for thinking of her and for trying to be a wordsmith.

This is a good ongoing gesture. It will probably go a long way toward getting you out of the doghouse.

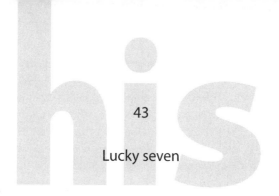

43

Lucky seven

for this gesture, you'll need a medium-sized gift bag, tissue-grade gift paper, a bamboo plant, a four-leaf clover, a horseshoe, a rabbit's foot, a Buddha statue, a penny, and a number seven, such as the kind you'd use for a mailbox.

She's up for a promotion at work, the lead in a play, or a top-ten finish in a marathon—maybe all three at once. You can say, "Good luck" or "Break a leg," but that's really pretty lame. Talk is cheap. She wants to feel like you really *mean* good luck, like you're genuinely in her corner and pulling for her with all your might. If she doesn't, she'll assume you're a typical male, jealous of her success or turning her accomplishments into competition. But you're much more enlightened and sophisticated than the average Joe, right? Give her the gift of good luck—in fact, give her a whole bag of it.

Round up the above seven items, which are said to bring good luck. If it's the dead of winter, you may have to settle for a picture or drawing of a four-leaf clover. If she's a member of People for the Ethical Treatment of Animals, you may want to substitute the rabbit's foot with a doll, and tell her the doll represents lady luck. You should be able to find the horseshoe at an antiques and collectibles store. Once you've rounded up all seven of these lucky items, put them in a gift bag, which you can buy at any greeting card store. Put the items in the bag, and surround them with the tissue-grade gift paper. Then, on the eve of her accomplishment, give her the gift of extremely good luck. Tell her you wanted to do more than simply wish her the best. If she doesn't collapse into your arms, she's got a heart of stone.

This gesture is good just prior to her working toward a significant accomplishment: a new, better-paying job; a part in a play; or just before her first marathon.

44

Kiddie pool

for this gesture, you'll need to buy an inflatable or plastic children's pool, sunscreen, and some pool toys. If you're so inclined, you'll also need a blender, tequila, ice, margarita mix, and some of those little drink umbrellas.

It's hot enough to fry eggs on the driveway . . . if that's how you like your eggs. The mercury is about to bust through the top of the thermometer. Your chili dogs are turning into hot dogs. You get the picture: It's the heart of summer, and it's sweltering. Someday the company you've started will go public, and you can buy a summer home on the Alaskan peninsula . . . or at least an Olympic-sized swimming pool for your extensive backyard. But until then, you've got nothing but a few scraggly trees casting shadows that wouldn't offer shade to a chihuahua. Not to worry. You can create a summer wonderland in your backyard for the two of you to enjoy.

Visit your local, friendly mega-department store, the kind that sells everything from groceries to time-share condominiums. This Taj-ma-commerce is bound to have a huge selection of inexpensive children's pools for the backyard. Find one that suits your needs and budget—just make sure it's big enough for two. Next, find some pool toys: swimming goggles, inflatable whales, beach balls, etc. Grab a tub of heavy-duty sunscreen, unless you want to invest in one of those collapsible gazebos. Buy a compact disc of Caribbean music. On your way home, stop by the liquor store and pick up everything you need to make frozen margaritas. Don't forget those little drink umbrellas . . . nothing says "paradise" more than useless miniature pastel umbrellas made out of wood and tissue paper.

When you get home, set up the pool. Throw in the toys. Get out the blender and mix up some industrial-strength margaritas. Crank up the stereo, put the speakers at the window, and let that steel-drum music repeat endlessly. Let her help you with this preparation, so she can get in the spirit as well. Slather each other up with sunscreen, and hit the pool. It's not quite the Bahamas, but it will do until you can afford the real thing.

This gesture is good for the heart of summer.

45

Turn-down services

for this gesture, you'll need new sheets and pillow-cases, a goose-down comforter, air freshener in a scent she likes, her favorite candy, and her favorite magazine or newspaper.

One of the nicest things about staying in a fine hotel is maid service. You don't have to feel guilty that you're not lifting a finger to help your significant other, and she gets to feel like a queen because someone else does all the cleaning. And the *pièce de résistance* in truly swanky places is the nightly turn-down service. Picture it: fresh linens, turned down to expose snow-white pillows. A chocolate mint sits atop one of the pillows like a gift from a truly mixed-up tooth fairy. Sometimes the establishment will even add a daily newspaper.

Provide her the same type of luxury in her own home while giving her a gift she'll enjoy. The bad news? You play the maid in this scenario. But she'll appreciate this gesture so much that you won't mind. First, buy her a new set of satin or high-thread-count sheets, matching pillowcases, and a feather-soft comforter. After you've put them on your bed, turn down the sheets and comforter. Spray an air-freshener scent she likes over your new creation. Put her preferred candy and magazine on her pillow. Then wait for her to find the surprise, you suave, debonair devil, you.

This is a great Valentine's Day or anniversary gesture.

46

Palace in the sand, message in a bottle

for this gesture, you'll need to be at the beach. You'll also need an empty wine bottle and—if you can find it—a piece of blank parchment paper.

The beach itself is romantic: the crashing waves, the breathtaking sunsets, the laid-back atmosphere. But just because you're on vacation doesn't mean you get to be lazy when it comes to making her feel loved and appreciated. No way! The sensuousness of the beach will put her in the mood—often—so the least you can do is reciprocate with some romantic gestures designed just for a tropical paradise.

Learn when low tide will fall—it's usually printed in the local newspaper. When the sea is at its ebb, go several yards up from the breaking surf and build the best sandcastle you know how to construct. Is it a dribble castle with tall spires? One made from pre-formed plastic molds? Humps of shapeless, sandy grit?

It doesn't matter. Do the best you can. Surround it with a heart that you scrape into the sand. Leave enough room to write a message to her. But don't stop there. Scrape additional messages in the sand all around your little kingdom—the more the better. Make them loving, make them racy. It doesn't matter as long as you perform this gesture close enough to shore that your citadel and sentiments will be washed out to sea. Nothing is more romantic than a loving gesture that's impermanent *and* time-consuming.

But wait! There's more! In advance, prepare one final piece of this gesture. Take an old wine bottle with a solid-fitting cork, add a loving message on a piece of fake parchment—or just regular paper if that's all you've got—and *voila*! Instant message in a bottle. Hide the bottle in the bathroom, and when she returns from admiring the palace in the sand you've built for her, run her a bath. When the tub is nearly full, toss in your bottled message. You won't need to constantly refill her mai tais to get lucky that evening.

This gesture is good for your summer or tropical vacation.

47

Very intimate messages

all you need for this gesture are a pen, a light touch, and a roll of toilet paper.

There's not much in life that's certain, but you can count on going through several sheets of toilet paper in an average day. And she uses even more than you do. Since she lacks the equipment to pee standing up, she uses a healthy wad of toilet paper to cover the seat of any porcelain throne that looks the least bit unsanitary. After you've done the standing-up deed, you tap. She wipes. The less said about the other necessary function in life, the better . . . but it does require some significant outlay of toilet tissue. In its pristine—or no-longer-pristine—state, there's nothing romantic about a roll of toilet paper dangling from a fake-chrome dispenser next to everybody's favorite seat in the house. But you can change that.

The next time the roll needs to be replaced, do something special before you replace it. Take a virgin roll, carefully unravel it, and write notes to her along the roll. If you so choose, make it one continuous string of messages. Be clever, write messages like: "And you said I was afraid of intimacy"; "Look out below"; "You're my number-one gal." Add some genuinely romantic sentiments as well. When you're finished, carefully put the roll back into its original condition, then put it on the holder, and wait to hear laughter echo from the tile-covered walls. Oh, and one more thing will make this gesture absolutely complete: PUT THE SEAT DOWN. Make it a habit. Consider it the essence of being a gentleman.

This gesture is good for any time.

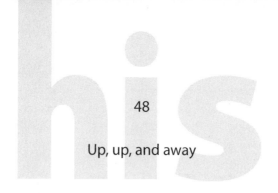

48

Up, up, and away

this gesture will work if you live in or near a medium or large city that has companies offering hot-air balloon rides. Rates for flying high in the sky will vary. A cheaper alternative is taking her to the top floor of the tallest building in town or hiking to the top of a nearby mountain peak.

You promised you'd take her to the top, and you've tried to deliver. You've got a good job, so you've bought her only the best. You've got artistic talent, so you've painted her a masterpiece. Now it's time to get literal and take her to heights that thin the blood and make the heart beat faster. There's a variety of ways to make hitting the heights a reality.

If you live in a medium-sized or large city, it's likely to have at least a couple of companies that offer romantic rides in a hot-air balloon. Airplane flights can be romantic, of course. You can pretend to be international smugglers or jet-setting celebrities as you join the Mile High Club. But nothing makes you feel the awesome wonder of flight quite like a ride in a balloon. You can really *see* how far below that hard ground is. You can shake your head at the folly of keeping nothing but a big ball of canvas between you and certain death. It's a thrill, and unless she gets faint standing atop stepladders, she'll love it too. Consider it moderately expensive, thrilling foreplay among the birds, the bees, and other flying creatures.

If you haven't quite reached the top of your profession—or it's one of those careers that makes you rich in experience but cash-poor—then you can opt for other ways to take her to the top of the world. That medium-sized or large city probably has its share of skyscrapers. If you're lucky, one or more of them will have a free observation deck or at least a place for the public to congregate and gawk at the ground far below. If all else fails, pack a picnic lunch, and take her to a local high-rise hotel. Take her to the top floor and sit near the set of windows that are nearly always next to the elevators. It's not exactly paradise, but at least it's unique.

If you're both nature lovers, you might consider taking her to the scenic heights. Hike up a mountain and sit at the crest of a waterfall or sheer rock face. Find the tallest hill in a nearby meadow and take her—and a bottle of wine—to the top of the knoll. Wherever you decide to take her, once you're there, say something like, "I promised you that if you stuck with me, I'd take you to the top. This is how I want to start. I love you." Whether you're in a balloon, a building, or on a mountaintop, she will appreciate your efforts to reach the heights together.

This gesture is good for any time. If you go the hot-air balloon route, however, you might want to make this a Valentine's Day, birthday, or anniversary gesture because it will be moderately expensive.

49

The perfect candidate

for this gesture, you'll need to write up a romantic resume, and create fake letterhead on fine paper.

Job-searching sucks. There's just no way around it. You go, figuratively, door to door, having those doors slammed in your face. You feel like a prize bull or cow awaiting a blue, red, or white ribbon at the county fair. And she's probably got it worse than you. No matter how enlightened society has become, prospective bosses will probably consider her personal assets as much as they will her professional ones. If she's out there slogging along that demeaning job-search trail, try to lighten the load she's carrying.

After she's spent hours in front of the computer crafting her resume, make up another one for her, one that will boost her confidence and self-esteem. Under "objective," write something like: "Selfless, caring, beautiful woman seeks mate who will be supportive and loving throughout the job-search process." In the experience section, you could write that she's had "Years of experience putting up with the opposite sex" or "Has provided comfort, love, joy, companionship, intelligent reasoning, and integrity to the man who loves her." For "awards and honors," include some of her traits you treasure: "Most likely to support her man when he's feeling insecure and unable to cope"; "Best at loving selflessly"; "Most likely to succeed at anything she sets her mind to." Leave this resume at a place she'll find it the next morning, just before she heads out to pound the pavement once again.

Complete your gesture by mailing her an acceptance letter. On resume-worthy paper, create a letterhead featuring a bogus company like Special People Inc. or Best Woman on the Planet LLC. Then write something like: Dear Ms. (her name here): After careful consideration, and after reviewing one million other applicants, we have decided to offer you a full-time, lifelong position because you are—quite literally— one in a million. Please accept our offer and begin immediately.

This gesture won't get her a "real" job, but it should lift her spirits as she goes about the process of finding one.

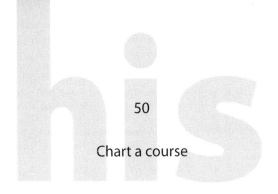

50

Chart a course

for this gesture, you'll need to consult your local college's noncredit course catalogue. Then you'll have to invest some time and a little bit of money.

Even if you live way out in the sticks, there's bound to be a junior college, regular college, or even a university within easy driving distance. Yes, they're filled with giant-sized, immature rug rats, but these schools *are* fountains of knowledge, information, and inspiration. If the two of you sometimes feel that you don't have much in common—or, more likely—she complains sometimes that the two of you don't have much in common, then one of these institutions of higher learning may be just what you need.

In addition to offering job skills for America's future and for those downsized by American industry, colleges and universities have what are called non-credit courses. As the name suggests, these aren't the variety of classes that push students one step closer to graduation. They don't offer credits toward graduation. They're classes you can take for fun to learn about subjects that interest you. If the thought of being back in a classroom makes you break out in a cold sweat, don't worry . . . Most noncredit courses don't have pop quizzes, twenty-five-page papers, or final exams. Exceptions might be language courses. You're not going to learn Swahili if you don't study and write down a few translations. And if it's a course about a literary figure, you'll be asked to read some of his or her works. But if you decide not to, you won't have your knuckles rapped by the professor. You'll just look clueless.

Stop by the college or university's information desk and ask for a noncredit course catalogue. Take it home and look through it together. Find a subject that appeals to both of you. Maybe you'd both like to be better chefs or learn how to cook dishes more exotic than Hamburger Helper Southwestern Style. Take a culinary course together. Or you've always thought it would be interesting to play handball. There's probably a noncredit handball course in the catalogue. You might also consider taking a course together about a subject that's never crossed your minds: Native American culture, the novels of William Faulkner, interior design, Esperanto. If you take a class in something foreign to both of you, you'll learn and grow together—and isn't that really what you're after anyway? You may discover that you've got a soft spot for poetry or Indian cuisine.

The cost of noncredit courses varies, as does the duration of the courses. If you look, you'll find classes both of you can agree on that fit your budget and schedule. Be open to exploration. Consider taking a course that interests her that sounds stupid and pointless to you. Exploration together is one of the keys to a healthy relationship. You can always take a course that interests you—and not her—next semester.

Fall and spring typically offer the greatest range of noncredit courses, but some are likely to be available in the summer as well. Basically, you can begin looking into this gesture at any time of the year.

51

Little things

items you need for this gesture will vary.

If you've skipped around and tried some of the ideas suggested so far in this book, congratulations. You're already more evolved than most of your Y-chromosome-bearing brethren. You're making the effort to brighten her life through romantic gestures great and small. Maybe you've invested an entire game day to do something just for her. Or you've increased your ability to recognize and meet her needs. Or you've learned something new about her, something that's made you fall in love with her all over again.

After you go above and beyond for her in the pursuit of romance, don't make a common guy mistake: thinking that one big gesture completely fills your romance bank account for the foreseeable future. If you think that way, it's completely understand-able. For better or worse, you probably look at being romantic the same way you look at a stack of paperwork on your desk: It's a problem to be solved through swift, focused action. Be romantic or cut down that pesky stack, and bam, problem solved.

Romance isn't a problem. It's an essential element of your relationship, and it must be cultivated constantly. That doesn't mean you've got to take her on a hot-air balloon ride, write sonnets on the bathroom mirror, or suffer through an opera every day. It just means you need to be mindful of all the little things that pop up daily, and make a habit of attending to them. Before you know it, these small gestures will become automatic.

1. Put the seat down. You can do some of your business from a vertical position. She can't. And nothing will wipe out the good will created by a romantic gesture faster than her nearly falling into the toilet after she's arrived at it, groggily, in the middle of the night, without thinking about the seat position, and you've left it up. If it makes you feel better, put down both the seat and the lid. That way, both of you have to lift something before you attend to the call of nature.

2. Listen, don't solve. When she gets home from work and complains about her job, don't try to give her solutions to the problems she mentions. She's a smart person. She knows, for example, that bad luck at work will turn around soon because of her abilities. She knows that she needs to talk to her colleague about the issue that's causing friction in the office. She's not complaining because she wants you to be a big, strong man solving her problems for her. She just wants you to listen sympathetically. Even if you think her issues are silly, they're real to her. They're valid. If you try to solve them, you're invalidating her feelings, even though that's not your intention. If she really does want your advice on how to handle a situation, she'll ask for it.

3. And while you're at it, talk to her. You probably don't focus on feelings. You focus instead on finding solutions to your problems. So you keep your feelings bottled up inside. She can sense this. She loves you, and she's sensitive. She knows something's going on inside your head, and it scares her when she doesn't know what it is. Tell her. Vent to her the same way you'd vent to a sympathetic colleague. In fact, *don't* vent to colleagues. It's bad form. Save up your grievances and share them with her. She'll appreciate you opening up, and you won't create ill will and bad karma at the office.

4. Be neat. She's not a maid, and she's not your mother. You're a grown man who takes responsibility seriously. Don't throw your clothes in a heap on the floor, waiting for her to come through and pick them up. After you eat, rinse your plates and silverware, and put them in the dishwasher. If you eat a bag of potato chips in front of the television and leave crumbs everywhere, vacuum them up. Rinse off your nasty, grime-filled toothbrush on occasion. You don't have to be a neat freak. You just need to show common courtesy.

5. Control your less-pleasant, though necessary, bodily functions. There's not much you can do about these equations: beer + consumption = belching, and junk food + consumption = farting. These are natural functions. But don't make them a *magnum opus*. You can belch the alphabet? Great! Do it for your buddies, not for her. Go to the bathroom to do these things, or at least into another room. It's just common courtesy.

6. Don't drink right out of the carton or bottle. You don't have to cooties, but it's still kind of gross for you to take out that carton of orange juice and suck back a hit right out of the spout. You know you're just trying to conserve a clean glass, but she doesn't look at it that way.

7. Groom yourself. If you're clean-shaven, be clean-shaven. Don't let the stubble grow just because it's Saturday. She hates the way it feels when you hold her close. And if you've got dirt under your fingernails, clean them. Nasty fingernails gross her out. Could you weave a sweater from your nose hair? Invest in an electric trimmer.

8. Yield the remote. You like to think of yourself as the king of your castle, and the remote is your scepter. Don't be a bully. Abdicate your throne on occasion, and hand her the remote. You've got more than one television in the house, right? Let her have the big one with the stereo-surround system. Bone-crunching tackles won't be quite the same on a smaller screen, but you can experience your share of them another time. Better yet, STAY in the living room with her when she puts on a show she likes.

9. If you chew, throw away the can or cup containing your sputum. 'Nuff said.

10. Say the words: I LOVE YOU. You do love her, right? She knows you do, but she still wants to hear you say those three little words. They're like magic. If they don't come naturally, practice them until they do.

Oh, and one more thing . . . Don't make a big deal out of little things. Don't draw attention to the fact that you're doing any or all of these little gestures, because that will cheapen your efforts. She's perceptive. She'll know you're trying to mend your evil, guy ways.

now it's your turn . . .

. . . now it's your turn . . .

hers

simple and sexy things to do
for the one you *love*

sɪɥ

Nicole Murn Hayes *and* **Justin Cord Hayes**

Adams Media
Avon, Massachusetts

Published by Adams Media, an F+W Publications Company
57 Littlefield Street
Avon, MA 02322
www.adamsmedia.com

ISBN: 1-59337-479-8

Printed in Canada.

J   I   H   G   F   E   D   C   B   A

Library of Congress Cataloging-in-Publication Data
Hayes, Justin Cord.
His/hers : simple and sexy things to do for the one you love / Justin Cord Hayes
and Nicole Murn Hayes.
p.   cm.
Includes bibliographical references and index.
ISBN 1-59337-479-8
1. Couples—Miscellanea. 2. Man-woman relationships—Miscellanea.
3. Love—Miscellanea. 4. Marriage—Miscellanea. 5. Creative activities
and seat work. 6. Flip books. I. Title: Simple and sexy things to do for the one you love.
II. Hayes, Nicole Murn. III. Title.
HQ801.H3717 2005
306.7—dc22
2005021921

This book is available at quantity discounts for bulk purchases.
For information, please call 1-800-872-5627.

dedication

Nicole would like to dedicate this book to her amazing grandparents, Josephine and John Matarazzo. Their marriage of sixty-three years has been an inspiration to me, and I am grateful for all their blessings. According to them there are three key points to making a marriage last: communicate with one another, respect one another, and love one another. This book is also dedicated to my brilliant husband, Justin Cord Hayes. The amazing way he puts words together for a fun and interesting read is, in my mind, brilliant! I cherish him for the hard work, love, dedication, and understanding he gives to our son, Parker-John, and me.

acknowledgments

Nicole would like to acknowledge Paula Munier, without whom this book would not have been possible. Special thanks to our editor, Jason Flynn, and Adams Media. I would also like to acknowledge God for whom all things are possible.

her contents

∽⊙∈∾

4

6

Diamonds Aren't Always
a Girl's Best Friend

you're probably saying to yourself: What are you talking about? Of course diamonds are a girl's best friend. Diamonds bring a twinkle to your eye, when your significant other cannot. However, diamonds can't give you backrubs, kill spiders, or open jars. When he is happy, content in his masculinity, and feels like he has solved your problems . . . Boy, is life better or what?

It is truly rewarding to be with your significant other when you both click, are on the same page, on the same level intellectually, and can talk and communicate and make each other laugh. That's when he is your best friend and diamonds don't compare. Diamonds are supposed to be forever, but when both of you are using your minds, hearts, and uniqueness to have a romantic future together, that's what really lasts.

Most of what you will read about are gestures that require very little money or none at all. Since the

majority of us have no money (especially if you have kids) these ideas should be pleasing to your budget. So, how can you be more romantic to him? There are a number of ways you can bring more romance into his life, creative little reminders of the passion you hold for him. You may even manage to wean him off of a constant stream of televised sports.

1

Waking the bear

the only items you'll need for this gesture are coffee, a coffee maker, and the ability to get up a little early.

Before you hit the snooze button that second time, get out of bed and make him his coffee. If you are a modern woman—independent, strong-willed, and believe that you were not born to be a servant girl—consider the cup of coffee a gesture of love.

If he's like most men, he's a bear in the morning and *must* have that coffee before he will even acknowledge your presence. But if you greet him with his kill-the-bear juice when he stumbles out of bed, adjusting himself and muttering under his breath, he'll perk up instantly. Be warned: You may get a hug and kiss for your efforts, so steel yourself for a blast of morning and coffee breath.

This is an ideal gesture for random mornings or mornings after he's had a particularly hard day at work.

2

Ding-dong. It's not Avon calling.

items you'll need for this gesture are a six-pack of his favorite beer, money for a pizza, and a little advanced planning.

Men love pizza, beer, and Monday Night Football. It's part of their genetic makeup. You can make Monday special for him by purchasing in advance a six-pack of his favorite beer and hiding it in a place he'll never look . . . where you keep the cleaning supplies, for instance. Put it in the refrigerator after he goes to work. Also, find out how much his favorite pizza costs and have a check ready for it. Plan to be absent for this gesture because your absence will make the gesture seem magical.

If he has a regular work schedule, phone in his pizza so it will arrive home just after he does. If his schedule varies, give him a call and find out when he'll be getting home. Don't worry. He won't get suspicious. He'll just think you're trying to keep tabs on him.

When he comes home, have the check and a note waiting under the remote control, which you've put in a conspicuous place. On the note, tell him you love him and want him to have the best Monday ever. Tell him to expect a knock at the door soon, which will be accompanied by a pizza. Inform him of the beer awaiting him in the fridge. It will be too early for Monday Night Football, but he can always heat up some pizza later. Come home after you're pretty sure he's gotten his pizza and is into his second or third beer. He will kiss your feet.

This gesture is perfect for Mondays during football season, but it can be done anytime. Plan it for a night when his favorite television show is on, for example.

3

Chalk up some romance

items you'll need for this gesture include driveway chalk, getting off work a little early, and the tiniest bit of drawing talent.

Get home well before he does and cover the driveway with chalk scribblings, just like you did when you were a kid. The only difference is that this time you're covering the driveway with drawings and words of love. If he's had a hard day and he's as observant as most men, you'll need to do something to draw his eyes to the pavement—otherwise he'll completely miss your romantic gesture.

Leave a couple of pails of chalk at the front of the driveway to block it, for instance. At first, he'll grumble. He just wants to get out of the car, go through the door, and collapse in his favorite chair with the remote control. But once he sees what you've done, his face will break into the same grin he used to carry around

when he was sizzling ants with a magnifying glass. Invite him to add his own artistic and poetic ramblings to the driveway.

You might have some fun and make your driveway art a gentle reminder of chores that need his attention. Men fear the dreaded "honey-do list": Honey, do this. Honey, do that. But if you can draw his attention to overflowing garbage pails with drawings that also remind him of how much you love him, he'll be more likely to be at your beck and call—even before he's had that I-just-got-home martini.

This gesture is good for any day, especially if the skies are clear for days to come.

4

Ice cream in bed

you'll need all the makings for his favorite ice cream treat for this gesture, and you'll need to be able to put them all together first thing in the morning.

This is a twist on breakfast in bed, perhaps the oldest romantic gesture in, um, romancehood. There's no law that says breakfast has to have eggs or bacon. So break out the vanilla ice cream, hot fudge, whipped cream, and cherry. Make a towering sundae and wake him up with it one Sunday morning.

Make it more than just your average hot fudge sundae. Cover the ice cream with conversation hearts or little heart sprinkles. And if you're in the mood, you can find some other creative things to do with that whipped cream . . . or with the cherry on top.

This is a great gesture for the weekend. It's a perfect way to remind him—and you—of how to be a kid again.

5

Objects of love

for this gesture, you'll need an extra-long lunch hour and some creativity.

Plan to meet him for lunch one work day, at his favorite place. Bring with you a box or gift bag. When he asks you what's in the bag, tell him it's a bag of your history together or that it's a box of romance. Smile at his blank or confused expression for a moment, guide him to a table, and fill him in.

Before meeting him, put into the box or bag anything that reminds you of your love for him or your history together. For example, if he makes you laugh, you might put a picture of a clown in the box. If he makes you feel safe, you could represent that by a toy sheriff's badge you pick up at a department store. If you spent your honeymoon in Disneyland, mark that with a Goofy figurine. Make sure you explain that the figure does NOT suggest you think he's goofy, or

you will offend his fragile male sensibilities. Instead of describing what each object or picture in the bag means to you, you could include him by seeing if he can guess what the pictures or objects represent.

This gesture is good for workdays or weekend picnics, or it could be a prelude to "real" anniversary gifts.

Sowing the seeds of love

for this gesture, you'll need seeds, garden supplies, and a green thumb.

Grab some flower seeds and plant them so they'll grow into the message "I ♥ U." This is a romantic gesture that will last an entire season and return every year—if that green thumb of yours is working. It will surprise him as the words start to appear, and it will surprise you if it actually works.

This is the sort of gesture you might appreciate more if he did it for you, but it's the little things that add up to enhance your romantic relationship. Men love how mysterious women can be, but over time that mystique can grow fainter. Keep him on his toes with surprises and your mysterious side, so he'll always want more.

This gesture takes time, but it will be a long-lasting testament to your love for each other.

Making a game of romance

for this gesture you'll need poster board, magic markers, a ruler, glue, scrapbook supplies, and your imagination.

It's not always easy for you to tell each other what you consider romantic or what you like in the bedroom, so why not make a game out of it—literally? This gesture takes a lot of preparation, but the rewards—for both of you—are worth it.

On the poster board, draw out game spaces. Be creative and use the scrapbook supplies—or pictures cut out of magazines—to fill in the spaces. Write down a list of questions to ask each other that correspond to the spaces on the board. You can use one set of questions or a "his" and "hers" set. It's up to you. Questions could be: What less-than-obvious part of your body is an erogenous zone? What would you like me to do to that part of your body? How do you like your kisses?

Open-mouthed wide? Short or long? Tongued or sweet? Wild and fast?

This game gets you talking about intimacy and sex in a "nonthreatening" way. You know how embarrassing it can be to tell him you'd like more foreplay or that his kisses are too wet? Well, this game gives you the opportunity to get more out of intimacy and lovemaking. The best part is: He'll think you're doing this for him, but . . . the benefit for you will probably be greater.

This gesture is good for anytime, especially if your physical relationship has been flagging lately or you are just getting to know one another.

Eat off his accomplishments

items you'll need for this gesture include that stuff he keeps in various places all over the house that remind him of his "illustrious" past. You'll need poster board and some scrapbooking supplies. If you also have a laminating machine, that's great. But you can get laminating done at any copy store.

Most guys like to brag about their past. If yours is no exception, then he'll have, for example, newspaper clippings of the day he made the winning touchdown in high school or tickets stubs from theater productions in which he starred, or better yet, the ticket stub from seeing his favorite band after standing in line all day for the tickets. Chances are, your guy has his memorabilia strewn throughout the house or stuffed in a closet somewhere. Since women are more detail-oriented, it's up to you to gather the record of his important achievements.

One of the best ways to ensure this stuff isn't just hidden away in a box is to create placemats out of it. Cut the poster board into placemat shapes; then get creative. Put the memorabilia onto the placemats, along with appropriate scrapbook stickers: footballs, comedy/tragedy masks, whatever. Once you're finished, laminate the placemats, so they'll be permanent testaments to his past. He'll appreciate the time, effort, and thoughtfulness it took for you to complete this gesture. You can also take this memorabilia to a copy store where they transfer it onto the color copier. Then they can laminate it for you into a placemat.

This is a great gesture for his birthday or any other time when he's likely to think about his glory days.

Baby, you can wash my car

you'll need super deluxe car-wash solution, top-grade car wax, interior protectant, and some elbow grease for this gesture.

You're the most important thing in his life . . . unless he's focused on his car. Then it feels like you're a distant second. Why are cars so important to men? It's an ancient mystery that dates back to troglodyte days. Cave paintings are sure to exist that show Og, rising and adjusting himself, spending Saturdays polishing his wheel. If you lavish attention on your chrome and two-tone rival, then he will temporarily associate you with his car. This is a good thing . . . most of the time.

One weekend day, when he's engrossed in college or pro football—or taking an undeserved weekend nap—go out and detail his car. "Detailing" is basically the same thing as "washing," except that it's tons more expensive if you have it done professionally.

First, wash the exterior of his car with the finest washing solution money can buy. For that, follow the recommendation of someone at the nearest auto supply store. Buy some of that special stuff that's supposed to be just for cleaning tires. Really make his ride sparkle. Pay close attention to the wheels, bumpers, and any other chrome-looking parts.

After you've washed his car from top to bottom, wax it. One way to make this easier is to buy an electric polisher/buffer. It's one purchase he will not complain about . . . Girl Scout's honor. Buff his car until you could eat off of it. Then attack the inside. Vacuum it first, then cover anything that's not glass or carpet with protectant. It cleans the interior and makes it shiny. Detailing also involves cleaning the parts of a car's interior that are sometimes overlooked—all the cracks and crevices, portions of the interior that are underneath the seats. If you don't want to go to that much trouble, it's OK. Just washing and waxing the car will be enough to make him spend most of halftime singing your praises and professing his undying love to you . . . until the third quarter starts.

This gesture really is a labor of love. It will take some time. Save it for a weekend after he's been particularly sweet, or after he's achieved something, like a promotion at work.

Making love from nothing but bills

for this gesture you'll need your checkbook and of course money in the checking account, a little time, some stamps, and a card you picked out just for him.

If you're living together, you're probably the boss of bill-paying. Guys aren't usually detail-oriented, and bills are just too much for most of them to handle.

Turn this less-than-pleasant chore into an overture of romance. When you pay that next bill, use it as an opportunity to send him an uplifting card at work. . . . He just might get it in the nick of time, at a moment when he really needs an encouraging word. After all, businesses rarely recognize or motivate hard-working, honest employees—so someone has to!

This gesture is great at the time of the month when you're the bill-paying maven. He'll appreciate a loving card arriving at work, no matter what kind of day he's having.

Playing hooky

all you need for this gesture is a sick day and the courage to claim it.

A relationship can sometimes suffer because both of you are so busy with what you think of as your "real life"—working forty or more hours a week. Even the best career path has stones and stumps strewn along it. If you've gotten to a point where you don't reach out to one another anymore, enduring those bumps in silence instead, then it's time play like a kid holding a thermometer up to a 100-watt bulb. It fooled Mom into letting you take a day off from school. In a word: PLAY HOOKY, baby! Oops, that's three words. But you get the picture.

Play hooky together. Call in sick. Conjure up a couple of realistic-sounding coughs as you tell your respective bosses of the horrific maladies that have befallen you. Then get ready to spend the day

together, doing whatever you want to do . . . within reason. Neither of you should do housework or work of any kind, but if you want to "work on" each other, then by all means, get down to business.

Focus on each other and bring out that little kid inside of you. Go to the park if it's a beautiful day. Play Frisbee. Have a picnic. Drink wine out of bottles in paper bags. Swing each other on the swings, and then go see a movie. Seeing a movie is the perfect activity for your clandestine day of fun and excitement. You don't have to worry about somebody from work seeing you out when you should be sick in bed, and you both will likely have the whole movie theater to yourself.

Don't overdue this gesture. Make it an annual, or at most semiannual, occasion . . . and only after you've been giving your employers 110 percent for months.

Welcome home

for this gesture, you need your front door, timing, patience, and some tongue biting. While this one is probably best for folks who have been together for several years, it should work equally well for any couple.

You like to communicate. It's your nature. Talking is a way of establishing intimacy, blowing off steam, and to have your emotional needs met. That's why, as soon as he comes home, you want to tell him what the neighborhood bully did to your son today, how Jane needs new shoes, and how the toilet doesn't work. Right?

But men are odd creatures. When they first open the door, they have reverted to their ancient, Cro-Magnon counterparts. They want to go into their caves and huddle and gain strength. They feel like they've spent the day doing the modern equivalent

of hunting, gathering, and slaughtering wooly mammoths. The last thing they want is more challenges to face when they get home.

So, meet him at the front door all smiles and kisses. Grab his coat and briefcase, and tell him how excited you are to see him. Say nothing more. If he talks about how his day went, just listen and offer sympathy. If it was a bad day for him, validate his feelings with words like, "I know how you feel." He will be suspicious at first. But once he realizes you aren't doing all this because you've got *really* bad news to share, he'll relax. He'll probably even hug and kiss you and . . . miracle of miracles . . . ask you about your day and actually listen. He'll be ready to hear about the toilet.

This gesture is a good one for workdays. Make it a "just because" gesture. He'll appreciate it most if he's not expecting it at all.

Wall of love

for this gesture you'll need a sane mind if your garage is cluttered to the hilt, cleaning supplies, some organization, garbage pails, dust cloths, photos, magazine cut-outs, paint, and some creativity.

Most men like to tinker in their garage on various things, ranging from motorcycles to broken-down cars and fly-ties. How about showing you love him by making more space for him in the garage *and* painting it with your love to boot? To do the painting, your garage must at least have Sheetrock up. It's not going to be much of a picture if your canvas is nothing but wall studs.

First, straighten up the garage. Don't touch the stuff you know he uses often because he'll pay more attention to what's missing than to your romantic gesture. But take all of that other stuff—broken Christmas ornaments, ancient calendars featuring bikini-clad

women, those fifteen half-empty bags of potting soil—and find some shelf space for it. Or lug a couple of boxes up to the attic. After you organize the garage, paint one side of it . . . unless you're up to doing the whole thing.

Add poems you've written to him on the freshly painted wall, and put up photos of your moments together. Paint his favorite football team logo on one part of the wall. Put up pictures from magazines that remind you of him. Just be as creative as possible. Then wait for his face to light up the next time he goes out to tinker on his Hog.

This gesture will take some time, so you should probably do it on a weekend. If possible, find an excuse to get him out of the house for several hours. Give him tickets to a local college football game, for example.

14

Bubbles away!

for this gesture, you need a clean bathtub, bubble bath, bath oil, rubber duckies and other bath toys, candles, and music.

You love to soak in a hot bathtub filled with tension-releasing suds, right? Well, even though he would never admit it, he does too. You can make his day by having a bubble bath ready for him when he comes home from work or a day of golf with his buddies. Prepare the bath the same way you like it: aromatic candles everywhere, gentle music playing, tons of suds, and soothing bath oil. Bring out the little boy in him by adding to the bath a bunch of bath toys. After you've made him nice and relaxed and set his senses ringing, he'll probably want to add one more thing to the tub: you.

This gesture is good if he's been complaining of stress at work or just after he's finished a big project at the office.

15

Cable your love

for this gesture, you'll need to be able to afford cable television or a cable upgrade. You'll also need to visit or call your local cable company. You'll also want to purchase a universal remote control, a six-pack of beer, a big bow, and a length of ribbon.

Sometimes you may wonder which he loves more: you or the television. Or the remote control. After all, he hands you that sacred object about as regularly as Halley's comet passes the Earth. He spends more time grunting at football or basketball than he does having conversations with you. And sometimes you think you'd die happy if he lavished one-tenth of the passion on you that he does on Sunday's big game. If you can't beat these first loves, then join 'em: Buy him cable. Or, if you already have basic cable, get him an upgrade.

Chances are, you've already got cable. Most men believe it's one of the inalienable rights granted by

the Constitution. An upgrade, to one of the premium movie channels for instance, usually costs less than ten bucks a month. If he has a favorite sport, chances are there are cable upgrades that will give him even more games to watch. To top off this gesture, get him a universal remote control, if you don't already have one.

The best way to give this gift is to have it added on a Friday, without him knowing about it. Then, on Saturday, get him out of the house. Ask him if he'd rather help you clean the bathrooms or run to the nearest home-improvement store. He'll be headed for the door before you've finished the question.

While he's gone, tie a ribbon around the remote and put a big bow on the TV. Put a chilled six pack in a cooler at the foot of his favorite chair. Then wait for him to get back. He may be grumbling, but once he sees the ribbons, bow, and cooler, his demeanor will quickly change. After you tell him what you've done, he'll kiss you and hug you and maybe even be willing to cuddle for a full five minutes—an eternity by guy standards. Enjoy it. Once he turns his attention to his new present, he'll forget you exist for several hours at least. But on a visceral level, he will now connect you with the TV—which is a good thing.

This gesture makes a good holiday or anniversary gift.

Straight eye for the cute guy

things you need for this gesture are: money, knowledge of local spas, antique/furniture stores, thrift clothing stores.

Did you know there's a wealth of consignment, thrift, and antique stores where you can find quality clothing or furniture at really low prices? The best stores to go to are in the nicer parts of town because the quality of the clothing and goods is more likely to be upscale. Go to one of these stores to find him a whole new outfit. You could even buy some cologne if they have his favorite—*his* favorite, not yours, ladies. Replace his torn-up khakis and camouflage jackets with slacks and a sweater or even a shirt and tie. If he balks at wearing them, tell him that you brought his picture to the store with you. Say that the sexy blonde behind the counter said he'd be totally hot with this new look.

Then go to the consignment furniture store and find him something new for his favorite room. Get him something tasteful, something to counteract his poker-playing dog portraits and velvet Elvises. If he has tons of knickknacks—fishing lures, antique tools, golf paraphernalia, or cowboy movie ephemera—try to find a nice shelving unit he can use to display his manly totems. Chances are, the only source of light in his favorite room is a lava lamp or neon beer sign. So, get him a nice floor or table lamp.

If you still have money in your pocket, get him an appointment for a pedicure at your local salon. Make sure you set it up for him, because chances are he would never go to the spa on his own, if you just gave him a gift certificate. If he scoffs at the idea of a pedicure—saying it's not manly—then tell him pedicures were second only to vodka martinis on James Bond's list of favorite things.

This gesture is good for the holidays, when you're likely to be attending or throwing tons of parties.

Bumper your love

items you need for this gesture are: a make-it-yourself bumper-sticker machine, some creativity, and a few bucks.

You know those bumper stickers on the back of his car that create a montage of billboards for tailgating drivers? You know the ones: "Bass Players Know How to Finger," and "Horn broken. Watch for finger." You can—politely—get rid of them and also pronounce your love for him with this gesture. Create your own bumper stickers and cover up those grimace-inducing ones.

Kid havens like Chuck E. Cheese usually have machines you can use to make your own bumper stickers. When you make your stickers, be clever. Say something like, "Sorry girls I'm taken," or "I'm not this fast in bed," or "I am loved by a beautiful woman."

This gesture is good as a "stocking stuffer," or for any time.

Pet escape

for this gesture, you'll need your pet, yarn or string, magic markers, and poster board.

Your relationship is still in the early stages, and you've decided it's time to take a big step: You're going to introduce him to your first love . . . your pet. If Fido or Fluffy can sit still for a minute, then add this idea to your romantic repertoire.

Prior to the introduction, create a sign to hang around your pet's neck. Make it eye-catching and risqué, if you have an intimate relationship. For example, if you have a dog, the sign ought to say something like, "I love to lick balls." If you have a cat, "Good pussy" is appropriate. If you're still only at second base, the signs can be G-rated: "Love my master, love me," "Will work for table scraps," or "Don't forget I'm her first love, bucko."

When he walks you home, leave him outside for a minute. Grab your dog or cat, put the sign around its

neck, and get ready for that Kodak moment or funniest home video. Tell him to come in because you'd like him to meet someone very special. When he walks in and sees the sign, make sure you get his reaction on film.

This gesture is good if your relationship is new. If you've been together for a while, then you can adjust it slightly. If he never does his around-the-house chores, then make a sign that says, "I KNOW you're going to clean the toilets today."

19

Stick 'em

for this gesture, you'll need Post-it notes and his favorite book or work materials.

If he's like most men, he brings his work home with him every day. Or he spends time with his nose buried in books to help him further his business knowledge. You probably wonder sometimes if you should be jealous of all those pages, if they constitute "the other woman" in his life. Remind him of who deserves to make up the vast majority of his every waking thought by putting little notes throughout his book: "I love you," "Hi, remember me," and—if you really want to put a smile on his face, "Hi, can't wait to see (insert the name you give his most important manly part) tonight."

He will be surprised to see these little romantic notes throughout his book, and they're sure to make him smile. After a while, he'll probably start hunting

through every book in the house to see if you've put notes in them as well. Go ahead and do it, just don't make them time-sensitive bits of information. And don't write something when you're mad and stick it into the family Bible or something. He may wind up reading it after he's been a total sweetheart for several days, and the note will just cause problems. And finally, make sure you don't stick notes in business material he needs the next day for a very important meeting. It might catch him off-guard when he's laying out for the CEO his strategic plan to increase profit for shareholders by 20 percent, and out falls a note that says, "Hi, can't wait to see Big Pancho tonight."

This gesture is good for when you're feeling neglected in favor of his take-home work. It's a way to let him know how you feel without starting an argument.

20

Like beer for chocolate

for this gesture, you'll need to buy beer, cigarettes, or chewing tobacco—whichever he most prefers. You also should buy a bag of adhesive bows and perhaps some Post-it notes for messages.

You don't know why you love chocolate, but you do. You'd do almost anything for it. Most men can take or leave chocolate, but they will crawl across a room of broken glass to get to an ice-cold beer. Or, for some, a pack of smokes will cause them to brave blizzards. And—sorry—for some guys it's a big plug of chewing tobacco that will cause them to brave certain death. Some men like all three, but all men love at least one of these vices.

Even though the thought of kissing him after he has smoked or chewed or belched the alphabet can be pretty gross, sometimes he just needs to spit, puff, or chug away. Satisfy his oral fixation by buying

41

him a case of his favorite brew, a carton of his chosen smokes, or several pouches of his favorite chew. Put some of this bounty in expected places, but hide some of it where he's less likely to find it right away . . . with the cleaning supplies, for instance. Put a bow on these hidden goodies. You might even try to wean him off of these obsessions by putting a note on his beer or tobacco that says something like, "You don't need these. Let ME be your oral fixation."

This gesture is good for any time, especially if you've recently complained to him about his habits and decide to make up for it. Let him have his other loves, as long as they don't start to replace you in his affections.

21

Naughty and nice

for this gesture, you'll need new lingerie and panties for every day of the week.

If your romance is new, you can wear a potato sack, and he'll think it's the sexiest outfit he's ever seen. You can be in a pair of his tighty-whities, and he'll be overcome with desire. As time passes, sex often becomes less exciting. And if you've been married for a while, it can become a chore akin to paying bills, or a pleasant, though infrequent, diversion. If you want to bring lovemaking back to the forefront of your relationship, then appeal to the horny teenager that still lurks within him, buried under distracting adult responsibilities. Surprise him with new lingerie and panties for each day of the week.

Your local shopping mall probably has a couple of stores devoted to lingerie, and if it doesn't, most large department stores devote a major chunk of real

estate to intimate apparel. If money is an object—and you or a good friend has seamstress talents—take items already in your closet and give them a new look. Sew naughty sayings into your sexiest pairs of panties. Add new lace and trim to an old bra for a new look. Make sure he notices your new "outfit." Tell him you'll have another surprise for him the next day. It's sure to spice up your romance.

This gesture is good for any time, and it's going to be more effective for couples who have been together for a long time than for those just starting out. In the early days, you probably won't need to make any special gestures in order to make whoopee.

The child within

this gesture will require different items and activities, depending on what your partner liked to do when he was a boy.

Most likely, you still know how to find that vulnerable little girl who hides inside the body of a competent adult. She comes out whenever you're on the phone with friends, or when you're watching a favorite romance. But him? He may act childish from time to time, but chances are, he's no longer in contact with the little boy he used to be. He left that smiling, upbeat kid on the sandlot baseball field or on his high school gridiron. But within him—probably not even too deeply within him—that little boy is still ready to play. Lead him down the path to that younger self, and you'll bring more fun and closeness into your relationship. If you're still getting to know each other, you'll make that fire burn brighter. If you've been together

for a long time, you'll rekindle those flames. Find out what he liked to do when he was a child, without asking him directly. He may not have super powers of perception, but he'll wonder why you're asking a question about his childhood likes. If he thinks you're up to something, he probably won't stop asking you what you're up to until you break down and tell him. Men are good at screwing up your nice gestures. Don't let him do it. Call up his folks and ask them what he liked to do as a boy. Or call up one of his long-time friends. Failing that, tell him you need to get a present for your colleague's son. Innocently ask him, "What do little boys like to do?" Most likely, his answer will include the things that HE liked to do as a child.

Once you're armed with knowledge, re-enact what he loved to do as a kid. Was it flying a kite? Building mud castles? Playing baseball? Surprise him on your next date with whatever he loved to do as a boy, and you will bring out the child in him—and probably have some fun yourself. In addition, your gesture is likely to break down some of his defenses. You'll see sides to him that you never dreamed were there.

This gesture is good for when he complains frequently about the stress of work. Often, this is code for: I'm not having any fun. So in other words, this is good anytime.

Your love in black and white

for this gesture, you'll need to put a romantic classified ad in your local paper. And you'll need some Silly Putty.

A classic romantic gesture is to buy a classified advertisement pledging your love. Make it something sweet and romantic that reminds him how you fell in love with him. But there's a good chance he'll never see it. Men are not known for their powers of perception. You go to the hairstylist to get a whole new look, and he stands there, dumbfounded, vaguely aware that something's different but unsure of just what's changed. Besides, if he reads the paper, it's probably just the business and sports sections and a cursory glance at the front-page headlines. Unless he's looking for a new job, he won't be skimming through the classifieds. So put a twist on this romantic chestnut with one of your favorite childhood toys.

When your ad appears, make an imprint of it with Silly Putty. You remember . . . it's that pink stuff that comes in a plastic egg. If you put it on pictures or text in the newspaper, it picks it up. It's also the stuff that got you banished to your room after you experimented with what it might do if squashed into the living room carpet. Once you've copied your ad, stick it someplace he's sure to see it: on his briefcase, on the refrigerator, on his toolbox, on the lid of the toilet. Or buy several packs of Silly Putty, and put your ad all over the house. Once he's seen it and gotten a good laugh from its presentation, take the original ad and put it in your scrapbook.

This is a great "just because" gesture. It also can be one of your anniversary gifts or a present for Valentine's Day.

The Golden Rule of Love

for this gesture, you'll need a notebook and to do something nice—and unexpected—for him each day.

You'd love it if, every day, he did something to make you feel special. Duh. But how do you train him to give you that extra five-minute cuddle—or to get him to cuddle at all? By following the Golden Rule. You remember. It's the one that says treat others as you would like them to treat you. So, with this gesture, do all the things to him you'd like for him to do to you. And just to make sure he's paying attention, tell him in at the beginning of the week that you're going to do something extra special for him each day of the week. And all you ask in return is that he write down in a notebook what you've done for him each day.

For example, let's say you give him a foot rub or caress his bald spot with your fingers as he watches the game on Monday night. On Tuesday, meet him at

the door with a martini when he comes home from work. On Wednesday, buy him that laser level he's been raving about for weeks. You get the picture. At the end of the week, see if he's noticed all that you've done. If you're really lucky, he'll write down stuff that you do every day that he just hasn't noticed before. By forcing him to pay attention to the details, he'll appreciate you more. And he may even start reciprocating. So, you see, even though this gesture is "for" him, you'll be the one to reap the rewards.

This gesture is good for when you want to build your appreciation for each other, and it's worth repeating throughout the year.

Surprise date

for this gesture, you'll need a car, a bandana, some cash, and some planning. And if you have kids, you'll also need a babysitter.

After a while, the normal routine of daily life leaves you feeling like a robot. In the wake of bills, chores, and earning a paycheck, you no longer stop to smell the flowers. And you probably don't have as much fun with each other as you should. So, take him on a super-secret romantic evening, full of surprises.

Tell him to dress casually for the night because you're going out, and you're going to surprise him at each destination. Go to the car, get out the bandana, and tell him to put it on—no peeking. Oh, and make sure you're the designated driver for the evening. Take him out to eat, to the last place he'd expect. For instance, if he likes fine French cuisine, take him to Hooters instead. If he prefers Hooters, take him to a

five-star joint. After dinner, blindfold him and take him out for some old-fashioned fun: miniature golf, bowling, the skating rink, etc. Take him either to a place you know he'll like, or to a place you think he's never been. It's up to you.

End the evening by picking up his favorite dessert and taking him back home. Have him keep the blindfold on, so he won't know where you are. When you get to the driveway, hand him the dessert and see if he can guess by smell what it is. Then, tell him you're out at Lovers' Lane, and you're going to rock his world. If you're afraid neighbors will see what happens next, then take off the blindfold and say something like, "Would you settle for a night with a beautiful woman who loves you?" Then, take him inside and rock his world—after you've sent home the babysitter, that is. Once in the bedroom, have him put the blindfold back on. Then tease and tantalize him with a variety of sensuous scents and tactile sensations. Let the remainder of the evening surprise you both.

This gesture is good for Valentine's Day, your anniversary, or whenever you want to bring some extra spice into your relationship.

Christmas in July

for this gesture, you'll need to go into your storage area and bring down the Christmas ornaments and goodies. Buy some small gifts to serve as stocking stuffers. Trot out your favorite eggnog recipe and a pine-scented candle for additional atmosphere.

It's called the most wonderful time of the year, so why is the holiday season also one of the most stressful? You've got to make sure you send Christmas cards to everyone you or he has ever known, or you risk alienating someone for the entire year. You have to fight through bloodthirsty throngs of holiday shoppers, eager to pluck that last bargain before you can get to it. And then there are those endless holiday parties: his office, your office, your friends, his friends. Round after round of making small talk with total strangers whose names you instantly forget. It leaves you wanting to say, "Take your silver bells and shove

them where the Star of Bethlehem doesn't shine." Bypass the unpleasant aspects of the holiday season by celebrating Christmas in July—or whatever month you choose, as long as it's not December.

In the wee hours of the night, cart out your collected Christmas ephemera and decorate the living room with it. Skip the tree because that's too much work. But hang the stockings by the chimney with care. Put up some tinsel and garland if you feel like it. Festoon the rafters with sparkling lights. Take gifts you've bought him and put them in his stocking. When morning comes, get out the pine-scented candle and put it near his bedside. When he wakes up, confused at the out-of-season scent, yell, "Merry Christmas, sweetheart." Take him into the living room, serve him some heavily spiked nog, and make like it's Christmas morning—without the cards, annoying shoppers, and endless parties you don't want to attend. All you get is that special feeling of happy, carefree childhoods past, and a day to count your blessings together.

This gesture is good for the summer, especially those times when both of you are feeling overwhelmed by adult responsibilities.

Fungus feet

for this gesture, you'll need to visit a shop that specializes in bath and personal-grooming products. Get a home-pedicure kit. Also, visit a drug store and pick up an athlete's foot cure.

You really need to love him to consider this dangerous assignment: Operation Fungus Feet. If he's like most guys, he doesn't take care of his feet. He wears the same socks for days at a time. His idea of washing his feet is standing in the shower. He's probably had the same pair of tennis shoes since the fall of the Berlin Wall. Odds are, he's got athlete's foot as a result. So it's up to you to boldly go where your man has never gone before: those nasty feet of his.

Go to a shop and purchase a home-pedicure kit. It's likely to have lotions, potions, notions, and pumice stones. On your way home, swing by the drug store and pick up an athlete's foot cure. When he gets home

that evening, tell him you're on a very special mission to save his feet from himself. First, take him to the bathroom, and wash his feet in the tub. Fill it up just over ankle-deep, and make sure to add some sweet-smelling stuff to the water, since you'll be spending some intimate time with those feet after they're washed. Then take him to his favorite chair. Sit him down, and get to work. Use the pumice to smooth his collection of calluses. Sand down those gnarly nails. Put some soothing lotion over those barking dogs. Close your pampering session with the athlete's foot cure, and make him promise he will continue to use it as long as directed. Once he has non-nasty feet, cuddling will become much more pleasant.

This gesture is good for any time.

Voila! Ze hamburger!

for this gesture, you'll need to take him to the fanciest restaurant in town, so be prepared to spend some money. You'll also need to make arrangements with maitre d' and restaurant manager, which will probably require some heavy-duty tipping.

If he's one of those picky eaters, whose idea of fine French cuisine is a French dip sandwich at the local deli, then this gesture is perfect for him—and it's good for you as well.

Call up the restaurant you've always wanted to go to and that he refuses to set foot in. Talk to the manager and explain your situation. Tell him that you'd love to come to the restaurant, but your significant other refuses to eat anything but the simplest meals: hot dogs, hamburgers, pizza, etc. Tell the manager that you need his help to pull off a romantic gesture. Ask him if he can arrange for the chef to cook up a hamburger

and then put it on a serving tray, one of those with a silver cover, so that your significant other won't know what's on the tray. This is where the heavy tipping comes into play. If the manager is sympathetic, you'll still need to arrange this gesture with the maitre d'.

Tell your significant other that you're going to take him to a special place for dinner. He'll probably start whining, telling you to make sure it's not one of those "frou frou" places that doesn't have anything he can eat. Tell him, "Trust me." When you get to *Chez Swanke* and you're seated, tell the maitre d'—who's in on the secret—that you've already had the pleasure of ordering for you both. He'll let the waiter know what's going on. Now comes the fun part. Watch your significant other sweat and squirm, imagining a plate full of snails or fish eggs. And then, when the fancy covered trays arrive, watch his face when, instead of escargot or caviar, the waiter uncovers a hamburger prepared just the way he likes it. And *voila*! You get your fancy meal in the town's finest restaurant. And he finds "something he can eat" there.

This gesture is good for Valentine's Day, birthdays, anniversaries, or around Christmas . . . any occasion during which you're willing to shell out a little cash.

Significant Other's Day

for this gesture, you'll need green pipe cleaners, crepe-paper streamers, scissors, safety pins, green flower tape, and ribbon with his name on it.

Pick a day to honor him. There's already Mother's Day, Father's Day, Boss's Day, Veterans' Day, and a host of others. So, why not Significant Other's Day? To mark the occasion, make up some paper roses, similar to the ones veterans' groups hand out on Memorial Day and Veterans' Day or that Salvation Army bell ringers distribute around the holidays.

Go to a local craft supply store. Pick up some green pipe cleaners and different colored crepe streamers. Some stores might have ribbons with names preprinted on them. If the store doesn't have these, then you can add his name to ribbon with some glue and glitter or a permanent marker. Cut the streamers into petal shapes, and make "flower stems"

out of the pipe cleaners. Attach a ribbon to the paper flower. Put a safety pin through the flowers, so people can wear them on their lapel. Then, hand out the flowers to neighbors, friends, and family, so that they can honor him on his special—and unexpected—day.

This gesture is good for any time, especially when you just can't find the words to say, "I'm sorry" or when he's been down in the dumps.

30

Techno-age love

for this gesture, you'll need to be at least a little bit savvy when it comes to computers, digital cameras, and cell phones. Of course, you'll also need to own or have access to a computer, digital camera, and cell phone.

In order to make ends meet, he probably spends more time at work than he does with you. He spends hours staring at his computer screen, sifting through boring reports, perusing future projections, and—when the boss isn't looking—surfing the Internet or playing solitaire. Even if he's got a picture of you on his desk, he's probably more focused on the screen than he is your pretty face. In addition, his cell phone rings constantly with clients asking the same annoying questions. If you call him, he's likely just to act annoyed because he was hoping you were that one client he's been playing phone tag with for days.

One day, arrange with some of his colleagues to get him away from his computer for a few minutes. Once he's gone, download from a digital camera onto his computer photos of yourself and of the two of you. Then make the photos his new screensaver. Leave before he knows you've been at his office. Then, the next time he's sitting at his computer staring into the screen, bemoaning the rat race, your pictures will pop up, reminding him of the reason he works so hard . . . to spend money on you, of course! Seriously, the sight of the two of you on vacation or holding each other close will be a pleasing alternative to projections and reports.

Another day, when you're both home, set up his cellular phone, so that it will have a special ring whenever you call. If your service provider has "your song" available, then use it. If not, pick a love song, or a goofy song that will make him smile, like "Sugar, Sugar" by the Archies. That way, he'll know it's you calling during the day, to get his mind off that unreachable client.

This gesture is good for any time. You should arrange to change the photos and the special ring from time to time.

Romance survival kit

for this gesture, you'll need a toy stethoscope, a match, Hershey's chocolate Kisses and Hugs, a penny, and an inexpensive watch. Be creative, and add additional items to this list. You'll also need something, such as a plastic freezer bag, to gather these items.

There are times when you'd swear that the romance in your lives is like a seriously injured patient rushed to the emergency room: Flatline! We're losing him! Come on! Come on! No! He's gone. Oh God! It never gets any easier! The next time you fear the romance in your lives has died on the table, bring it back with a romance survival kit.

Go to a department store and gather the above items. Each is designed to be a gentle, light-hearted reminder that the distance between you has grown uncomfortably great. And let's face it, girls. The gulf is most likely there because he is a man, wrapped up in

himself and his job—not necessarily in that order—and romance isn't near the top of his priority list.

He probably grunts at—more often than he talks to—you. Your kit should contain a penny for his thoughts. He doesn't listen to you. He's too busy trying to "solve" your problems when you bring them up. Hand him the stethoscope, and emphasize that all you want him to do is listen. If it's winter and you were wearing white shoes the last time he held you really tightly and lovingly kissed you, give him the match to light his fire, and the chocolate Kisses and Hugs to guide his actions. And if—like most men—he's unable to be on time, get him a watch. The key to this gesture is offering it with a smile on your face.

This gesture is good for those times when distance has grown between you, and you want to try to bridge that gulf.

His favorite magazines

for this gesture, you'll need to get a subscription to a so-called gentlemen's magazine.

Men are visually stimulated. And it doesn't matter how much he loves you. He'll notice other women, and impure thoughts will run through his one-track mind. Gain some control by getting him a subscription to a men's magazine.

You may wonder, "Why would I want to give my guy magazines filled with pictures of beautiful, Amazon-breasted women whose headlights are always on and privates so sensuous?" Why? Because he'll love to get them and because it will show him that you are confident and comfortable enough with yourself to give them to him. Men love secure, confident women . . . and if he doesn't, then you're with the wrong guy.

Besides, providing him these visual stimulants will benefit you as well. They can only enhance your

foreplay (hopefully) and lovemaking. Finally, they'll make him more intelligent. After all, the main reason he reads these magazines is for the excellent short fiction and incomparable interviews, right?

This gesture is good for any time.

33

X-treme dating

for this gesture, you'll have to face your fear of incurring serious bodily injury.

Men love to flirt with danger. It's hard-wired into their impossible-to-understand psyches. When he was a child, he ruined at least one article of clothing each day in some harebrained scheme involving a tall hill, a feat of derring-do, and the chance to "show up" his buddies. Inevitably, these activities ended disastrously, with him ripping the seat out of his pants or the elbows out of his shirts. Yet, he never has learned his lesson, has he? The only difference now is that his toys are a little more expensive: mountain bikes, hang gliders, whitewater kayaks. Frankly, his passions—other than you— scare you to death. With this gesture, you can stare down that fear and get closer to him in the process.

The next time he engages in the death-defying endeavors he pursues, tell him you want to go with

him. He'll be shocked. He didn't even think of asking you because you've made it clear that near-death experiences aren't your cup of tea. Put on your best game face and say something like, "(Sky-diving, rappelling, kayaking in murderous whitewater) is important to you, and I at least want to experience it with you." And who knows . . . maybe there's some recessive death-defying genes buried within you that will emerge gloriously as you fly out of a kayak and into turbulent, turgid waters or fly over open space with nothing but a large kite between you and the rocks below. He'll appreciate that you're stepping out of your comfort zone to be with him, and it's bound to pull you closer together . . . if you survive the experience.

This gesture is good for boosting your confidence, so do it any time.

Glory days

for this gesture, you'll need to gather up all of the trophies and paraphernalia of past glories. He probably still has all of it around somewhere. If he has a championship ring, you'll need to pay to get it cleaned. You may choose to spend some money to frame newspaper clippings or to transfer old video footage onto DVD.

If he was a big star on the gridiron or diamond in high school or college, he's still proud of those accomplishments—regardless of his age. If he's like most guys, he could win the Nobel Peace Prize and still—in his heart of hearts—be more excited about that game-winning touchdown against the Waukesha Wombats all those years ago. If he received a championship ring for his efforts, he may still wear it regularly. And while he probably doesn't have his trophies, newspaper clippings, and videos of himself in action in a conspicuous

place, there's a shrine to them somewhere. Don't try to understand why those long-ago days mean so much to him. They just do. Show him that, even if you don't understand his obsession with ancient exploits, you appreciate that they mean a lot to him.

First, get his school ring. If he wears it every day, you'll have to be creative. You may have to purloin it from beside the sink in the dead of night and then feign ignorance when he's frantically searching for it. Get it professionally cleaned. Find all of those old newspaper clippings that feature him and that issue of *Sports Illustrated* that stars him in the "Faces in the Crowd" section. Find some nice frames and put all of those holy grails of greatness under glass, or you can pay to have someone arrange and display these items professionally. Finally, if he has videos of games in which he played, consider taking them to a shop where those videos can be transferred to DVD.

When you've got all of these gifts assembled, surprise him with them on his birthday or during the holidays.

You're on candid camera

for this gesture, you'll need cooperation from a local electronics store. You'll also need poster board and markers with which to make a sign.

Boys love expensive toys, even when they can't afford them. That's why he likes to visit the local electronics store . . . to drool over the latest television technology, to pant over the fanciest home theater equipment, to sigh over sky-high-priced sound systems. Consequently, you won't have any trouble getting him to accompany you to the electronics place. It's like a grown-up candy store for him. Make the trip special by publicly broadcasting your love for him on one of the big-screen televisions.

Call up local stores until you find one willing to work with you on this gesture. Here's what you're going to do: Make a sign for him with poster board and markers. Make it silly or fun, since it will be seen

by many folks. Go by the friendly electronics store and drop off the sign. The manager will make sure one of the shop's video cameras is hooked up to the biggest-honkin' TV in the place. Then go home and get him. Tell him you're taking him someplace special. When you get back to the electronics store, catch the manager's eye and cue him to position the sign in front of the camera. Your man probably won't realize what's going on at first, but once he does, he's sure to smile and be ready for his close-up.

This can be a great gesture for birthdays or anniversaries.

Guy movie marathon

for this gesture you'll need to go to your local video store and rent several movies.

Ah, an evening of movies at home ... wrapped in his arms, a romantic fire blazing, a shared glass of wine, the sights and sounds of machine gun fire and the snappy patter of fart jokes. The films you're watching might not be your first choice, but he loves them—guaranteed. There's a small pantheon of "guy movies," universally loved by those unfortunate enough to possess a Y-chromosome. If you can stomach an evening of them, you'll win his enduring gratitude, and he'll be less likely to grimace the next time you suggest taking in a so-called chick flick.

Give him a call at work one Friday, and tell him he's required to spend the evening at home with you because you've planned a movie marathon. You'll probably be greeted with silence or stuttered

protestations: "Sorry, hon. I, I, I've got to get . . . my . . . eyebrows waxed. Yeah, that's it. My eyebrows waxed." Tell him there's no ifs, ands, or buts. Unless he's really looking for trouble, he'll give you a "yes, dear." The stage is set. He's expecting to face an evening of smooches, awkward first meetings, and love triumphing over all. Instead, get him what he really likes: guy movies. The list may differ slightly from guy to guy, but you'll be safe with any of the following films: *The Godfather* (Parts I or II, not III), *Caddyshack*, *Animal House*, *Reservoir Dogs*, *Pulp Fiction*, any of the movies in which Clint Eastwood plays "Dirty Harry" Callahan, *Happy Gilmore*, *Blazing Saddles*, the Al Pacino version of *Scarface*.

When he realizes he's in for a night of his favorite flicks, he'll hug and kiss you and jump for joy. There's no telling what permanent damage an evening of stupid humor and violent retribution will do for you personally, but it will do your relationship a world of good.

This gesture is good for a Friday night, when you want to spend the evening with him but don't feel like going out.

Back to nature

for this gesture, you'll need a picnic basket, a pair of bikes, and a picnic lunch. You might need an oil can, an air pump, a blanket, bungee cords, or a backpack.

If you're like a lot of couples, you've got a pair of bikes gathering dust in the garage and a never-used picnic basket someone gave you during a long-ago holiday season. Finally, there's probably a spot only a few miles away that passes for the heart of nature even if you live in the hub of an urban jungle. Put these elements together for a romantic afternoon.

After you've slept in on a day off one pleasant spring or fall morning, send him up to the attic or into the storage closet for that picnic basket you've probably never used. In fact, you've considered palming it off to someone else as a wedding present . . . admit it. But you've held onto it because—deep in the recesses of your mind—you've planned for just such a day as

this. Put together a picnic lunch. Keep it simple: sandwiches, a couple of bags of chips, a chilled bottle of wine or soda. Then send him out to the garage for those bikes that haven't seen action since the dot-com bubble burst. He'll probably have to climb over perilous piles of rubbishy paraphernalia to get to them. Do you have an air pump? You'll probably need it. An oil can? You might need that as well. If he complains about having to be the one to extract the bikes, remind him of the possibility that spiders have set up time-shares within their spokes.

Once you have your fully stocked basket and your bikes dug out of the garage, it's on to whatever passes for nature in your neck of the woods. Hopefully, you've got a rack on the bike that can hold the basket and blanket. If not, put it in a backpack, and let him wear it. He'll feel manly carrying the load. Head off to the park or a nearby wooded vacant lot, or if all else fails, the empty parking lot of a business that's closed for the day. Then spend leisurely time enjoying your lunch after you've worked up an appetite from doing real, live, outside-of-the-bedroom aerobic activity for the first time in months.

This gesture is good for those times when the rat race is making you feel like glorified pieces of cheese.

for this gesture, you'll need to know what he most loves to do. You'll also need some paper and a pen.

Every weekend it's the same thing. He just wants to sit on his, um, assets and relax in front of the television with a cold one. But you need him to do some things around the house that he's promised all week to do. You try, politely, to make some requests of his time, and he grunts or stares like an armchair troglodyte. So, you resort to the dreaded (for him) honey-do list: Honey, do this. Honey, do that. You leave it on the dresser by his wallet, in hopes that he'll see it and do something worthwhile during your days off together. But there's something you need to know: He hates that list. Loathes it. Detests it. The next time the weekend rolls around, substitute it for a honey-do list he'll love. He'll appreciate your gesture because it makes him

feel that you trust him to get the around-the-house jobs done, even if it is in his own (sweet, slow) time.

Write up a list that tells him only to do the things you know he loves to do. If he's a golfer, tell him he needs to do you a favor and go play nine holes. Tell him to rent a golf cart while he's at it. If fishing is his passion, tell him he needs to pick up a few new fly-ties and head for the nearest stream. He likes to hang out at the local watering hole with his buddies? On your list, tell him he's not to come home until he's bent an elbow at his favorite pub. He won't believe his eyes, and best of all, he'll do anything you say without complaint for at least the next few days. He'll probably even be willing to follow a real honey-do list to the letter the next time he sees one, so this gesture will benefit you as well.

This gesture is good for a weekend when he's complained about being stressed. It will give him a psychic boost, and you'll receive the dividends.

Photo booth

for this gesture, you'll need to find a photo booth and have plenty of dollar bills. You'll also need to find a place that can laminate items for you.

If he's a reader, he spends so much time with his nose in a book that you wonder if he remembers you exist. And when he's really engrossed, he can flip pages during a Category 5 hurricane. But there's an easy and fun way to remind him of the important place you hold in his life: bookmarks. He's always look-ing for them, right? He'll use anything: magazine sub-scription cards, gum wrappers, bent pages, maybe even dollar bills. Replace those assorted scraps with photos of you.

Find a photo booth, the kind that gives you four poses and then instantly spits out the results. Your local mall probably has one. If not, you're likely to find one at a place that caters to kids: a pizza parlor with

performing robot animals, a complex that features go-carts and bumper boats, miniature golf courses with castles painted in shades of fluorescent pink. After you've located a booth, make sure you have plenty of dollar bills. Feed them into the machine, and get strip after strip of photos made. Make sure you vary your poses: sultry, silly, sexy, sophisticated. After you've collected at least a half-dozen of these photo strips, head to a copy center because most of them have laminating machines. Get your photo strips laminated, so they will be durable.

Once you've gotten your photos laminated, return home, and replace whatever half-torn paper he's using for bookmarks with your photo strips. If he reads multiple books at once, replace the makeshift bookmarks in each. Make sure you do this when he's not looking. Then, the next time he picks his favorite tome off the nightstand, he'll find your pictures. He'll have to think about you, at least until he returns to the naughty adventures of Nellie and Nina, or whatever it is he's reading.

This gesture is good for a time when you're feeling ignored. It's a gentle, fun reminder that you deserve to be the center of his attention.

Sunday funnies

for this gesture, you'll need the Sunday comics section of your local newspaper.

Admit it. The first section you turn to in your local paper on Sunday is the funnies. Who wants to get yet another eyeful of crimes, misdemeanors, and celebrity scandal? Not you! Well, maybe you'll glance back later at the celebrity scandal. But first, a giant cup of java and your favorite cartoon shenanigans. Meanwhile, at the other end of the couch, there he is, absorbed in abstruse box scores, sense-reeling statistics, and the latest exploits of guys who get paid way too much to play games for a living. It's a time of comfortable silence, when the two of you are together, but in your own worlds. Well, next Sunday, make those worlds collide.

Use the funnies to communicate about relationship issues you've not addressed during the week.

Even if your relationship is purring along like a contented kitten, there will be things said, things not said, actions taken, and actions not taken that are burbling away under the surface of that placidity. Bring them out into the open in a gentle way, before they rumble up into explosions. Go over to him with the funnies, open them up to a cartoon featuring two people, or two animals, or a person and a talking animal—the key here is two characters. Put words in one of the character's mouths. For example, if he tried to cook dinner for you a few nights ago and it was a disaster, and you basically suggested it was a disaster, then have the character say something like, "I sure appreciated you trying to cook me dinner Thursday. I had a rough day at work, so I didn't respond to your efforts very well." Hopefully, he'll catch on to what you're doing. He'll pretend to be the other character and say, "Sorry I used our fine china to catch oil from my motorcycle's crankcase. That sure was a silly thing to do." Continue in this vein. Don't be accusatory. Trust that by pointing out your own foibles, he'll respond in kind by making light of his own.

This gesture is good for clearing the air when there are minor issues dividing you. It's also just a good way to connect with each other in a fun way on a weekly basis.

41

Garage band

for this gesture, you'll need a guy who used to play music but doesn't any longer. And you'll need to find a storage center that allows bands. The ones in the heart of town are more likely to allow loud noise than those that are near neighborhoods. You'll also need to shell out some cash to rent a space at the center. If you can find posters of his favorite bands, then they'll make a great addition as well.

Does he treat the steering wheel, tabletops, and even his stomach as a drum set? Does he always have a lighter handy, in order to hold up it during an impromptu concert? Does he sometimes talk about how he "coulda been a contenduh," if only The Couch Potatoes hadn't broken up just because Jack got arrested and Stevie decided to get an education, when he should have known that it's *all about the music*? In other words, is he a frustrated musician? Does he have

a set of drums he never gets to play now that he's living a nice, quiet suburban existence? Or an electric guitar he has to play with his amplifier set to three instead of to eleven because the neighbors complain otherwise? You can evoke those days of yore, when he still had all his hair—in fact, it was heavy-metal-rocker long—and he still believed that he was going to score a record contract someday.

Most likely, your town has a number of monthly rental storage facilities. Some of them allow bands to set up their equipment and play, especially if they're far from suburbia, in the heart of the city. Call around, and find one that's open to someone occasionally rocking out until all hours of the night. Once you do, rent it for a month (if this gesture meets with his approval, you can always sign a longer lease later). Then, when he's away for several hours some evening, cart his musical equipment to your new garage away from home. You may need the help of some of his friends, especially one with a pickup truck. While you're planning all of this, see if you can find posters of his favorite bands. Or, failing that, go to some thrift stores and look through their boxes of cast-off vinyl record albums. Platters were still what mattered well into the 1980s, and you're almost bound to find albums by some of his head-banging favorites. Put up the posters or album

covers in the storage space, along with his drums or guitar.

Finally, set up a stereo for him to play along to, if he's a drummer. Or set up his amplifier, if he's a guitarist. Storage places that allow bands usually have at least a few sheds hooked up for electricity. Now, he's ready to rock! When he gets home, he's likely to notice right away that his instruments are gone. Tell him, "Don't panic." Tell him you've got a surprise for him. Then take him to the storage center, and let him relive days of tasty beats until he's limp as the hair of a heavy metal megastar who's been caught out in the rain. This gesture will allow him to breathe in a heavy dose of nostalgia, while also getting out some of his aggression. Perfect.

This gesture can be costly, so save it for a birthday or holiday gift.

Where have you been?

for this gesture, you'll need to hunt around antique/ collectible shops or go to an online auction Web site, to find old license plates from various states. You'll also need to go to a craft shop and buy a large corkboard, and you'll need some nails or heavy-duty thumbtacks.

There must be a "wandering" gene in men. They love to travel on the open road. For many, visiting new states gives them the same thrill troglodytes must have received from hunting and killing next week's wooly mammoth cutlets. And if he's lived in various places— especially if he's spent time in exciting locales like Las Vegas, Chicago, or New Orleans—then he probably finds ways to drop that information into conversations at office parties. With this gesture, you can help him relive pleasant memories of all the states he's called home.

Most antique/collectibles shops have at least a few booths with old license plates. Keep in mind that

you won't find them at "purveyors of fine antiques." You'll find them at places that sell "junktiques"—old odds and ends and castaway junk that others will consider timeless treasures. Comb through the old plates and find ones from the places he's lived. If there are a few you can't find, you can go to an online auction site to complete your collection. Or just keep digging around. It's fun. It becomes a sort-of treasure hunt, and you get to have the thrill of temporarily being a hunter/ gatherer yourself. Anyway, once you've collected all the plates you need, go by a craft supply store and buy a corkboard large enough for all the plates. And get something you can use to affix the plates to the board. When you get home, put the plates on the corkboard. If you know the order in which he lived in the different states, then put them on the board in that order. But if you don't, that's OK. Then, wait for a gift-giving occasion. But be warned . . . once he receives this gift, you're probably going to hear—for the umpteenth time—all the anecdotes about life in "Vegas, baby!" or good ol' times in The Big Easy.

This gesture is good for a guy who's settled down and has moments when he wishes he still had the freedom to spend extended stays in new places. It makes a good gift for his birthday.

43

Decked-out ride

for this gesture, you'll need to find all kinds of cheap, silly items with which to adorn the inside of his car. You can locate items at auto parts places, as well as department and dollar stores.

No matter how sensitive and urbane he might be, he's a guy. That means he loves his car, whether he's the anti-establishment type who drives an old Volkswagen Beetle, the nouveau-riche BMW fanatic, or the outdoors enthusiast tooling around in four-wheel-drive pickup caked in mud left over from off-roading adventures. Sometimes he lavishes so much attention on that damn car, you'd swear he'd marry it if he could. Express your jealousy in a light-hearted way that will make him smile—and focus on you for a change.

Go to auto parts places and department stores and look for all kinds of cheap, silly items for his car. For example, find a pair of the classic fuzzy dice, the

gaudier the better. Try to find them in pink. Hang up air fresheners featuring naked women, Tiki gods, and/or brilliant maxims like "Who farted?" or "Is it hot in here, or is it just me?" Encase his steering wheel in fake leopard hide. Just let your imagination go. When you're done, don't say anything to him. Just let him enjoy the thrill of discovery. Make sure you don't do this gesture the night before he has to pick up an important client first thing in the morning or after you've had a fight. If you've just battled, he'll take this gesture as an assault on his character. Otherwise, he'll see it as the humorous act it's intended to be. And who knows? He may decide he likes the pink, fuzzy dice, and they'll become a permanent part of his ride.

This gesture is best for when things are going well between the two of you, when your days are filled with laughter and joy.

Through the years

for this gesture, you'll need an object from each year you've been together.

When a relationship begins, every moment is special and charged with meaning. And each moment raises a host of questions: Does he like me as much as I like him? Do I really like this guy? What did he mean by that? Could he be the one? As time goes by, you still have special moments together. But they're a little fewer and farther between. It's OK. No matter how much Hollywood may try to make you feel differently, relationships in time stop being charged with erotic and romantic passion and become something comfortable. They become your bedrock, your unfaltering support system. And even though the growth is slower, your relationship remains an organic system, a work in progress. Relive some of those moments from your time together with this gesture. You should

already have everything you need for it, either placed in a storage box or out in the open, where you can see it and gain constant strength from it.

Find one object that symbolizes each year you've been together. It doesn't necessarily have to be something relating specifically to you. For example, if you're both sports nuts who cheer for the same ball club, you may have a pennant from the year your team went to and won the World Series. If you look at that pennant together, it brings back instantly for you the ups and downs, the triumphs and heart-stopping moments of that season that you shared together. But the object could as easily be a photograph of your first date or from your first trip together. Maybe the object is a newspaper announcing your engagement, or the stuffed gorilla he bought for you as an olive branch after your first major fight.

Once you've found the items that best symbolize each year of your relationship, assemble them. See if they have the same importance to him that they do to you. If they don't resonate with him, *do not* hold that against him. If he were to perform this gesture for you, he might very well choose items with which he fiercely connects that wouldn't mean much to you. This isn't a gesture of one-upmanship. It's an opportunity to relive your shared past. And if a particular item

doesn't hold any meaning for him, explain to him—lovingly and honestly—why it's so important to you. During this exercise, you'll come to know each other even better. Most likely, you'll create a new special moment together that you'll treasure.

This is a perfect anniversary gesture.

Say it with balls

for this gesture, you'll need brand new golf balls, some Post-it notes, and a gift certificate to his favorite golf course.

Men have always loved golf. The day is bound to come when archaeologists will discover new cave paintings that show prehistoric men of leisure holding sticks and aiming them at little round stones—to one side will be a rendering of Shorg the Cave Dweller sporting a green jacket. Why do men love this pastime they call a sport? The answer is shrouded in mystery. Maybe it's because golf is a popular game that does not involve sweat. Those who participate in this sport don't have to run up and down a court or be body-checked by a 300-pound offensive lineman. And it's a great form of macho male bonding that allows a guy who can't scrape two nickels together to feel like he's

part of a wealthy crowd. If he loves golf, then this gesture is for him.

Buy him new packs of his favorite golf balls, after you've bought him a gift certificate to one of your area's more prestigious public courses. Then write a series of messages on Post-it notes that clue him in to the fact that he'll be hitting the links soon: "Want to hit a few?" "Lost your balls lately?" "This ball was made for you," "Ready to putt it in the hole?" and "More balls where these came from." Put the notes on the new golf balls, and lay the balls in a line that leads him to the gift certificate. He will give you the most enthusiastic embrace you've had since the days when you were just starting to date.

This gesture is good for spring or fall, especially when he's been complaining about how stressful work has been lately.

Trading kids

for this gesture, you'll need good friends you trust, kids, some money, and planning.

Life comes at you pretty fast, and it seems like you never have time alone together anymore. After eight hours on the job, you come home to an endless list of chores, a heaping mound of bills, and kids whose egos have been bruised on the playground. It's easy to forget that the man you love even exists. If you're lucky, he's right there beside you lending a helping hand. But then you're more like coworkers than friends or lovers. Well, you're not alone. You have good friends going through the same situation inside their own frazzled American Dreams. You should consider making them an offer they can't refuse.

Make a commitment with some of your closest friends that you'll agree to watch one another's kids one Friday or Saturday each month. Most likely, you

won't have any trouble making such an arrangement because they're as anxious as you to feel like a couple again instead of like the CEOs of an often-thankless corporation. This is a win-win situation for you and your friends because you don't have to pay a babysitter, and you know you trust your friends to be there for you to make this commitment. Once you've made it, the two of you can go out and enjoy just being together.

This is a good ongoing gesture, provided you've got good friends in close proximity that are willing to agree to it.

Words and pictures

for this gesture, you'll need a large piece of poster board, scissors, glue, photos of the two of you together, an appropriate-sized frame, and stacks of your favorite magazines.

Running away from—or after—boys, recess, lunch, and making collages . . . these were your favorite activities in grade school. You remember. You took stacks of magazines, found pictures in them that "spoke" to you, cut them out, and put them on pieces of poster board or construction paper. *Voila!* Instant art that created a portrait of you, even if you had trouble drawing stick figures. With this gesture, you can evoke the nostalgia of those simpler days, while creating a romantic keepsake for him.

Buy a piece of poster board and a frame that will fit it, as well as scissors and glue if you don't have them. Next, gather up those stacks of magazines collecting

dust by the rhododendron. See, you knew there was a reason you hadn't thrown them away. Instead of creating a self-portrait like you did in school, you're going to create a collage that represents him. Cut out words that make you think of him: strong, sexy, goofy, fun. Cut out words that evoke your relationship: solid, special, romantic, dedicated. Among the words, add photos from the magazines: happy couples, favorite activities, preferred vacation spots. Finally, add some actual photos of the two of you. When you feel your masterwork is complete, put it in the frame. It won't be something to hang in the Museum of Modern Art, but it will be perfect for an office or cubicle wall.

This is a good gesture for Valentine's Day or for your anniversary. Consider updating it from time to time, by creating new collages.

48

A fortune in Kisses

for this gesture, you'll need several fortunes from fortune cookies, a bag of Hershey's Kisses, some aluminum foil, scissors, and lots of patience.

The best part of Chinese takeout is the fortune cookie, which distills the wisdom of the mysterious Orient into a pithy prognostication that always seems to speak directly to your situation. You've been feeling lately that no one appreciates your efforts at work? Then that's when you'll crack open the cookie and find, "Your effort will be rewarded handsomely." You're so stressed out that your anxieties have anxieties? Then you'll surely be greeted with, "You will soon take a magical trip," after you've scarfed down your moo goo gai pan.

You know it's silly to put any stock in the prophecies of junk food, but you just can't help it, right? Well, he can't either. But you don't just want to give him a

bunch of fortune cookies. What if one of them talks about "finding a new romance" or something? Here's a solution that combines fortunes you approve with a batch of sweet Kisses . . . the Hershey's kind.

Collect at least a dozen fortunes that reflect him or that command him to do certain things: "Be most affectionate today"; "Your humor is your strength"; "Love with passion." Then go out and buy a bag of Hershey's Kisses and some aluminum foil, if you don't already have some. Cut the foil into squares large enough to rewrap the Hershey's Kisses. Take the chocolates out of their packages, put the fortune cookie fortunes around the chocolate, and then rewrap the candy with the pieces of foil. Then, the next time you order out for Chinese, give him the batch of chocolates with your very own handpicked fortunes encircling them.

This gesture is good for any time.

Serving together

for this gesture, you need to find community or social projects for which you can volunteer, and you need to be prepared to devote several hours of time to hard work that doesn't pay a cent.

Life moves awfully fast, and it feels like there's only time enough to serve your own needs, and—if he's lucky—maybe some of his as well. But there's nothing quite like the satisfaction you get from helping others who are less fortunate than you. Or from doing something constructive for your community. When you've selflessly served others, you've contributed to something greater than yourself, and you realize that there's more to life than 9 to 5, household chores, and prime-time television.

If you serve others together, both of you get to experience that unmatched satisfaction. There are many avenues that lead to service. Call your local

United Way. This nonprofit organization is essentially an umbrella agency for a host of other nonprofits in your community. Typical agencies serve seniors, the mentally disabled, and the impoverished. Others may focus on hospice care or health issues. You might decide to give blood together for the American Red Cross, read to underprivileged children, or deliver meals to the elderly. Each United Way typically has an office devoted strictly to matching volunteers with a variety of service projects.

Other service projects can be found through houses of worship in your area. Most churches have outreach committees that offer service to those less fortunate in the community. Around the holiday season, you might wrap presents for underprivileged families. You might assist others in the congregation who are helping to build homes for Habitat for Humanity. Finally, you can phone city hall and find out if there are any community projects going on in your city: tree plantings, community clean-up days, toy drives, etc.

This gesture will bring you closer together, even as you help others or your community. It's good for any time of the year.

A romantic cereal

you'll need note cards, a pen, tacky gag gifts, plastic storage bags, and boxes of cereal for this gesture.

When you were a little girl, cereal was fun because it contained prizes. You would have eaten something called Kardboard Krunchies if it had contained a prize you wanted. You've never enjoyed cheap, chintzy trinkets so much since. For some reason, cereal makers don't add prizes to cereals that target grown-ups. What a shame. If you're going to have to choke down a bowl of pure, tasteless bran, couldn't the company at least reward you with, say, a tin whistle or some cool stickers? Admit it. If prizes came in adult cereals, you'd probably still take home the box that contained the best treasure. If he's a kid at heart—as most men are—he misses those prizes too.

Go over to your pantry and take a peek. There's six to a dozen half-empty—or half-full if you're an

optimist—cereal boxes in there. And not one of them is any fun. They're all reminders that you're not getting any younger, that you need bran and fiber, that sugar is an evil menace. Run, don't walk, to the drawer where you keep pens, note cards, and other odds and ends that you probably should throw away but never do: gag gifts from coworkers, tiny gifts from folks you barely know, junk you picked up at the last "business after hours" affair. Armed with this negligible booty, find some small plastic Baggies—the type too small for sandwiches but just right for a couple of handfuls of raisins or other no-fun snack foods that you force yourself to choke down.

Write love notes on the cards: "You're my favorite morning treat"; "A bowl of cereal, a glass of juice, and thee"; "Romance: It isn't just for breakfast anymore." Find a suitably silly "prize" from your stash of semi-abandoned junk, and put it and a note into one of the Baggies. Make up as many of these bundles as you have boxes of cereal. Then put them into the boxes when he's not looking. Wait patiently for the morning when your cereal-box prize falls out into his bowl. He should get a kick out of it, and he may even open up and talk about favorite prizes he's received in the past.

This gesture is good for any time.

Packin' the fridge

for this gesture, it needs to be cold enough outside to store most of the items in your refrigerator. You'll also need to pick up all of the junk food, beer, and other items you know he loves.

No one raids the refrigerator/freezer like he does. If it were an Olympic sport, they'd have to invent a new, higher-grade-than-gold medal for him: the stealthy slink, the rapid jerk of the door, the junk food disappearing as if by magic, the door closed again so rapidly it won't affect your electric bill. Sure, you try your best to put some stuff in there that isn't completely free of nutritional value. But he always manages to evade that stuff he calls "junk" and find the good stuff: beer ("We don't need no stinking lite beer!"), mega-caloric bean dip, chili cheese frankfurters ("Just heat and serve!"), microwaveable White Castle hamburgers, 40-ounce bottles of malt liquor, soft drinks, candy bars.

It's enough to make *you* sick, but he loves that stuff. So make him a deal. Tell him that if he eats at least reasonably healthy for two weeks, you'll reward him with a surprise that will make the extreme sacrifice worthwhile. See that he holds to his side of the bargain, without cheating too much. Plant spies, if necessary: coworkers, friends, your kids if you have some. He can be extremely clever when foraging for empty calories, so you may also have to resort to subterfuge. Keep watch like a hawk over the refrigerator. Take all the bad stuff in the pantry and hide it in places he'd never look.

When the two weeks are up, surprise him. Take all of the healthy items in the refrigerator and put them outside—if it's cold enough—or into a spare icebox if you have one. Then fill the fridge with all of his disgusting favorites. Get him every variety of carbohydrate-heavy, artificial-ingredient-rife, proudly empty-caloric junk food item known to humankind. Then wait for the expression of joy on his face the next time he opens the refrigerator door. Tell him not to eat everything in one sitting. Repeat this gesture, making the time between sacrifice and overabundance longer each time. With luck, he'll get to the point that he no longer craves the stuff he shouldn't be eating anyway. And, he'll think it's *his* idea.

This gesture is good for wintertime.

The whatever enthusiasts

the cost and materials for this gesture will depend on which pastime/activity you choose.

You have your little worlds, and he has his—and rarely the twain shall meet. While you focus on gardening or mountain biking or playing bass in a jazz combo, he's in the garage, building high-powered rockets or in his room reading the complete works of Gerard Manley Hopkins. Individual hobbies are great. They help you to forge your own, independent identities. They give you opportunities to have time for yourselves, a necessary ingredient in the strongest relationships.

But shared hobbies and pastimes are equally important. You can try showing interest in his interests—or introducing him to yours—but it's not likely to be successful. Dipping a toe into the pastime pools of one another's worlds adds spice, but too much of it can make you feel like you're losing your identities.

Fishing is *his* hobby. Shopping is *your* hobby. Avoid unhealthy competitive streaks by finding a hobby you can share.

There are bound to be interests that both of you have flirted with, without, um, going all the way. Both of you have a passing interest in interior design, for example. But your budget's tight. So, you could start going together to area thrift stores to look for gently used furniture and accessories that you can work on restoring and refinishing together. Perhaps you keep a journal, and he writes poetry. You can combine your love of writing by coauthoring a play. Turn the occasional stroll around the block into hiking up the side of mountains or taking up rock-climbing. The two of you might also consider taking up a hobby that seems alien to both of you. You're both couch potatoes? OK, take up scuba diving or rollerblading. You're so active you're only still when you're sleeping? Find a sedentary habit to share: needlepoint, painting, listening to the great operas.

The possibilities for finding a new pastime to share are limited only by your imaginations. Be open to his "outlandish" ideas, and tell him to open to anything you suggest that he finds off-putting at first. This gesture is a good one to start at any time. It will bring you closer together, even as you learn new skills or find strengths in yourself you never knew existed.

Secret code

the items for this gesture will vary, depending on what object or objects you use for your secret code.

It's universally accepted that men and women don't communicate well, but in truth, no two people will communicate effectively all the time. Even you and your best friends occasionally have misunderstandings or disagreements. If she's with a guy you think is all wrong for her, for instance, you'll probably veil your true opinions behind empty platitudes in order to spare your friend's feelings. But as your friend—and a naturally sensitive, intuitive woman—she'll pick up from your body language or expression that you're not telling her everything. If she's brave, she'll push. If you're brave, you'll be honest with her about your feelings, even if it will cause her to be angry with you for a while.

Life would be great if a series of spoken and unspoken messages worked the same way with him.

But men aren't wired that way. For better or worse, they understand something only if it's direct: a request, a demand, a straightforward question. Indirect questions, demands, and requests go right over their precious pointy little heads. And body language? Forget it. He'll probably sense something's wrong or that he's not responding properly to you, but he won't understand what you're trying to communicate. And after a while, he's likely to get frustrated and shut down.

The answer? Create a secret code you can agree on to deal with topics that cause tension between the two of you. For example, you love cuddling, right? He probably doesn't, unless he thinks it's foreplay. But there are times when even he's open to intimacy that doesn't end with flinging clothes to the four corners of the bedroom. How do you know when your worlds are aligned? Well, you could ask him if he's in the mood to cuddle. But chances are he'll say he isn't, even if he is. Why? Who knows? It's a guy thing. Don't try to understand. How do you get around this impasse? Choose a secret code. It could be a gesture or an object—a paperweight for him, a hair bow for you. When your bow is in a particular, preordained spot in the house, he knows you're interested in cuddling. Then he can feel it's *his* decision to "humor you." And when he's in one of those rare open-to-cuddling moods, he can

put his paperweight in the same spot. For this to work, both of you must agree not to get upset if the other *doesn't* respond to the secret code.

Devise other codes to detangle other thorny issues. He's slow to do his household chores? Then devise a hand gesture—no, not the one starring the middle finger—that tells him: "Honey, you may have noticed that there a number of things you need to do around the house, things you've agreed are your responsibility. And they haven't been done. I don't want to nag you, but I do want you to consider getting to those chores when you can break away from important stuff like scarfing down junk food or watching guys in helmets and body pads crash into each other." If he likes to have sex more often than you, find an object or gesture that says, "I'm ready for you, big boy. Come to mama."

Any time is a good time to initiate your very own secret codes.

Under the stars in your own backyard

for this gesture, you'll need camping equipment, provisions, and a backyard. You might also go to a craft store and pick up a wood-burning kit. You might need to call your local government and learn about the laws governing open fires on private property. If you make a fire, you'll need wood, sand, and matches.

Guys like to believe they're rugged outdoorsmen who could survive getting lost in the heart of the woods. It doesn't matter that he's a couch potato except for those weekends he goes off on hunting trips with his friends. During those weekends, he's a pioneer, an explorer, a swashbuckling adventurer cutting a broad swath through the great outdoors. If you prefer to keep the outdoors where it belongs—outside your nice, climate-controlled house—there may be a way to forge a compromise that will be acceptable to both of you.

Surprise him one weekend by taking all that camping equipment in the garage and setting it up in the backyard of your home. Be a pioneer yourself: Don't ask for help with any of the set-up. Figure out on your own how to put up the tent. Roll out the sleeping bags and air mattresses. Get out the camp stove and hook up the propane. Even better . . . find out what the local laws are for open fires. If necessary, invest a few bucks in a burning permit. Then lay down some sand, pile a stack of firewood over it, and make a good ol'-fashioned campfire.

If you're really creative, you can take one of the logs for the fire and use it to make a sign to place in front of your front door. At a craft store, pick up a wood-burning kit. It allows you to burn messages into wood. Take one of the logs—or just a plain block of wood, if you like—and burn onto it something like, "Camp Ruffin' It." If it's a log, put it in front of the door or at the entrance to your driveway. If it's a board, try hanging it on the front door.

Give him a call on his cellular phone and find out when he'll be getting home. Just before that, bring out the provisions: hot dogs, buns, baked beans, marsh-mallows, graham crackers, and bars of chocolate for s'mores. Put some beer in the cooler. When he gets home, he'll be amazed to see that you've shunned the

comforts of home for the call of the wild. Tell him, "I know you always want me to go camping with you, but I'm pretty much a homebody. So I thought I'd bring the campground to us." Then get ready to spend a romantic evening under the stars. Best of all: Your home is just a few feet away in case you forget something. And you won't have to pee behind a row of bushes. Who knows? You may like this experience so much that you're willing to rough it for real next time.

This gesture can be as simple or as complicated as you wish to make it. It's best for late spring or early fall.

55

Say it with balloons

for this gesture, you'll need balloons, scrap paper, pens, darts, thumbtacks, and a large corkboard.

Birthdays cease to be fun after you've reached a certain age. They just become days to mark—or mark out—on a calendar. You can expect sympathetic calls from friends and family. The expression "over the hill" ceases to be funny. You're not alone in dreading the anniversary of the day you entered the world. He may not admit it, but he's also feeling the sting of another year passing. It's just not manly to admit it. Once, he was the "golden boy" in his organization. Now he's the wise mentor. He used to be on top of popular culture. Now he doesn't recognize a single one of the "Best New Artist" nominees for the Grammy.

Even though he dreads his birthday as much as you dread yours, there's always that little ember glowing inside him that wants to have fun on his very

own day. He doesn't want another "grown-up" birthday observance. No way. He wants something that will make him feel like a little boy again. Nothing does that quite like balloons. Maybe it's because they're bright and lighter than air. But it's probably because they make a loud sound when they pop. Making loud noises that scare others—especially the fairer sex—is one of a boy's favorite pastimes.

For his next birthday, bring back some of those pleasant childhood memories by re-creating one of his favorite childhood carnival games. First, go by one of those industrial-strength-sized arts and crafts emporiums. Find a large corkboard or—if necessary—several small corkboard squares. If it's one large board, you can hang it up at home with a hammer and a few nails. If you're using several small squares, they will most likely stick to a wall with some of that gummy adhesive that doesn't leave permanent marks. If in doubt, ask a customer service representative at the shop. Then look for several bags of balloons in different shapes and sizes. The crafts store may have darts, but you'll probably have to go to a sporting goods or large department store for those.

When you get home, put the cork board or boards up on a wall in a room that's not as likely to receive guests—your bedroom, for instance. A game

room is ideal, if you have one. Next, prepare the balloons. On slips of paper, write love notes, love coupons ("The bearer entitled to one immediate roll in the hay"), riddles, jokes—basically, anything fun. Roll up the pieces of paper so they'll fit inside the balloons. Then blow up the balloons and tack them in rows on the corkboard. You're ready for the birthday boy. After you give him his "real" presents, give him one final gift. What's in the box? The darts, of course. When he looks at you, puzzled, take him to the room with the balloons and let him be a kid again. Chances are, no matter what "real" gift you got him, his favorite memory from this birthday will be the balloons.

This gesture is for his birthday. It's time-consuming, so you'd better really love him if you're going to do it.

Summer on ice

for this gesture, you'll need to take him to the local ice-skating rink in the middle of summer. Then pick up a wintry film at the video store. Make sure you've got hot chocolate in the house as well.

It's hard to think about winter sports when the thermometer is in danger of exploding from the heat. In the middle of a summer heat wave, the only skiing that sounds like fun takes place on the water behind a powerboat. What better time to visit the local ice-skating rink?

Make sure you perform this gesture on one of the hottest days of the year. Wake him up with a cup of hot chocolate instead of coffee. Be prepared. He may spew that first gulp across the room in surprise. Tell him he needs to pack a bag with warm clothes because you're going someplace chilly. Don't worry. You probably aren't giving away your destination. He's

a guy, remember? Subtlety is lost on him, bless his heart.

Make your trip to the rink a little racier by blind-folding him on the way to your secret destination. When you get there, enjoy some freezing fun. Even if you were an alternate for the Olympics, pretend you're having trouble staying on your feet. This will give him the chance to feel manly as he "helps you" skate. If he's all fumbling feet, don't laugh. Encourage him.

When you're done skating, go to one more chilly place: the beer aisle at your local grocery store. Let him pick up his favorite ice-brewed, *après* skate beer. Then swing by the video store and find a movie set in winter or in a perpetually frigid locale. Ignore *The Iceman Cometh*. It's not what it sounds like. Go for a Christmas film instead. Or *Fargo* if both of you like intelligent action flicks.

This is a good gesture for the heart of summer.

Twelve months of romance

for this gesture, you'll need a wall calendar, large squares of poster board, all-purpose glue, rubber cement, and scissors. You'll also need to take favorite photos to a local camera or copy shop and have duplicates made, unless you don't mind giving up the originals.

Every year, it's the same thing. He puts up some calendar featuring scantily clad women, fast cars, motorcycles, or all three. Maybe he's the type who puts up twelve months of inspirational sayings, or dopey cartoons. Whatever he uses, it probably doesn't remind him of you. Are you going to accept that? An object he consults nearly every day that doesn't contain a trace of you? No way!

Once the New Year begins, the price of wall calendars drops dramatically. Pick one up. It doesn't matter which one. You're not going to use the pictures in

it anyway. Next, go to an arts and crafts store and buy any of the following you don't already have: enough poster board to cover the photo pages of the calendar, all-purpose glue, rubber cement, and scissors. You're going to cut the poster board to fit the wall calendar's photo pages—you know, the ones above the rows of dates. Affix the blank poster board to the photo pages with all-purpose glue. Now you're ready to get really creative.

If you're an artist, then paint him a different romantic picture for each month. If you're a poet, write him a year's worth of romantic ballads. Or you can fill up the blank pages with photos of yourself and the two of you together. Get copies of the photos made, unless you don't mind parting with the originals. Customize the calendar any way you like. Just make sure it says, "Look at me, not the Playmate of the Month or the Very Best of the Muscle Car of the Month Club." When you're done with your creation, give it to him as a late holiday gift or remember-me gift.

This is a good gesture for the beginning of the New Year.

Test your love

for this gesture, you need access to the Internet, an open mind, and some diligence.

Are you made for each other? For centuries, there's been no sure way to answer that question. Women visited fortunetellers, read tea leaves, or consulted Tarot cards. But these methods were often inconclusive. And besides, the results were open to interpretation. Thanks to the magic of modern technology, you can find out— instantly and without question—if the two of you are destined to be one of the world's great romances.

If you're in the beginning stages of a relationship, there are a number of Web sites designed to augur your chances of romantic success. Just think! If Romeo and Juliet had had access to the Internet, they would be alive today. Or at least they would have died of old age, probably in completely different relationships that would have had much happier endings. If you really

want to find out how your romance is going, log on to *www.lovetest.com*. It will match you up based on your horoscope, personality, or numerology. It doesn't get more scientific than that. You can take a romance quiz at *www.pureromance.com* that will tell you whether or not you should cut your losses. Finally, Dr. Love can give you inarguable proof that your romance is a fizzle or a flame based simply on your names. If *www.lovecalculator.com* says, "No way, Jose," then he'll understand when you tell him, "We can't be together because Dr. Love says it just won't work out. It's better this way."

If the great Dr. Love gets you interested in learning more about the power of names, then visit *www.kabalarians.com*. The site uses mathematical principles to give you a free, brief, first-name analysis. It can be scary how accurately your name matches your personality. But that's OK. Use the Web site's logic to find a name that has a personality you prefer, then bam: you've got the character you always wanted. If you'd like a second opinion on your or his personality, you can go to *www.cooltests.com* to get free, general personality tests. If the personality and romance tests all work out to your liking, then you can use *www.virtualkiss.com* to send a digital peck.

This is a good gesture for when you're just getting to know each other.

Pizza pizzazz

for this gesture, you'll need to buy a large, frozen cheese pizza and—separately—his favorite toppings.

Maybe he's an aficionado of haute cuisine. But if he's like most guys, his favorite food is pizza. And why not? It's easy to eat in front of the television. Once it's cut, it comes in easy-to-handle individual slices. Almost anything can be served on it. And, best of all—for him—it's chock full of empty calories but has at least some pretense of healthiness. After all, it sometimes has vegetables on it. His doctor told him to eat more vegetables, right? He's just following orders. Why are you getting on his case? As food goes, however, pizza isn't very romantic. But you can change that with this gesture.

Buy a large, frozen cheese pizza. Think of it as a blank canvas. Then, go find his favorite toppings: Pepperoni? Pineapple? Slim Jims? These will be your paints

and brushes. The next time he's plopped down in front of his favorite game—and oblivious to all else—fashion your masterpiece. Use the toppings to spell out messages. Go for romantic ones like "I ♥ you" or "You are loved." No matter how tempting it may be, don't use this gesture as an intervention. Avoid putting messages on the pizza like, "Too many of these will kill you" or, "The doctor said no more cholesterol." Opt for using pepperoni and black olives to design hearts and flowers instead. When you give him his pizza, make sure he notices what you've done. He's engrossed in that game, remember? When he sees what you've done, it may actually take his attention away momentarily from the antics of guys with multimillion-dollar commercial endorsements.

This gesture is good for game day.

A tooth for a tooth

for this gesture, you'll need to reciprocate whenever he does something you like.

If he's been reading the other side of this book to learn ways he can please you with male-centered romantic gestures, you probably want to encourage him to continue. You can tell him how much you appreciate his actions, but that probably won't work. Instead, encourage him to be one romantic little devil by bringing out his competitive instincts. Nothing brings a guy to life like competition.

If he rubs your feet—without you begging— then encourage him to do it again by giving him a foot rub *and* a back rub the next evening. Don't tell him, "I'm doing this to encourage you to do more of what you did last night." Guys aren't good with subtlety, but they are always aware of competition. If he cooks you hamburgers and fries, bring home takeout

from his favorite sit-down restaurant a few days later. If he writes a sonnet for you on the bathroom mirror, then leave him love poems everywhere: his briefcase, his car, his toolbox, the drawer that holds the remote controls. If he does some of your chores for you without you asking, then do all of his *and* some that he's supposed to do but almost never does . . . like cleaning out the gutters.

After a while, he'll sense a pattern of one-upmanship emerging. If he asks you about it, be coy and tell him, "I'm sure I don't know what you're talking about. I just want to make you happy like you make me happy." But keep on "beating him" at the romance game. If he's got a Y-chromosome, he'll soon be going way over the top: buying you jewelry, taking you out to fancy places, going shopping *with* you without complaint. In a word, it will be paradise.

This gesture is good to begin at the first sign of his attempts at romantic gestures. Even if they're fumbling efforts, encourage him through competition. He'll improve quickly.

now it's your turn . . .